3·2·1

MARRIAGE

Leader Guide

3·2·1

Journey from vow

MARRIAGE

to VICTORY

JOHN & JULIE COLLIER

Leader Guide

SEMESTER 1

līfe
Bible Study

Birmingham, Alabama

321 Marriage—Leader Guide
Life Bible Study
An imprint of Iron Stream Media
100 Missionary Ridge
Birmingham, AL 35242
IronStreamMedia.com

Library of Congress Control Number: 2023941829

Cover design by twolineSTUDIO.com
ISBN: 978-1-63204-120-3 (paperback)
ISBN: 978-1-63204-129-6 (ebook)
1 2 3 4 5—28 27 26 25 24

CONTENTS

PREFACE

FOR THE LEADER

W e are so grateful you will be leading this study to help couples see marriage as God designed. God's blueprint for marriage is not just a topic we love to teach; it completely transformed our own marriage, as you will see in our story.

Practical Guidelines for Teaching the Curriculum

The entire content of the Participant Guide is in this Leader Guide; however, throughout this Leader Guide you will see ideas, suggestions, and further information provided for you. Beginning with the introduction below and moving through all the lessons, you will see the content for you set apart in a shaded box and in a different typeface. They are all designated **LEADER**. You will see some illustrations and more content that you may find helpful. However, you have complete freedom to share from your own marriage and life experiences, and to bring your own insight into each lesson as the Spirit leads.

Encouraging the Group: You will likely have couples at different places in their marriages (some vibrant and growing, some struggling, and some could be near crisis) and in different seasons (newlywed, married for years, blended couples, and so on). What all will have in common is the need to be encouraged and equipped.

Specific Practices: A few specific practices will be encouraged throughout the study and to be continued after it is over. They are:

- **Praying together daily:** You will see how vital this is for the study and for couples. As we have taught this for over a decade and a half now, this is the number-one thing couples later say to us that had the greatest impact then and continually.

- **A weekly "Starbucks moment":** This will be defined for the group in the curriculum, but it refers to a weekly time you get together as a couple to talk about things that are vital in your marriage. For you it may be a "Chick-fil-A moment," a "let's go for a walk moment," or something else that fits. The key is to have these regular meetings to talk about life and your marriage and to do so when you are not tired, stressed, or hurt. If this is not a regular part of your marriage, you can start now and include discussing things you are learning in this study.

- **The states of Intimacy—Conflict—Withdrawal:** Beginning in week 8, couples will learn the three states in marriage and how to move times of conflict toward intimacy and away from conflict. By this time, you will have had seven weeks with the group, so they should be far more comfortable sharing with the group and with one another.

As the leader/leaders, it's vital that you practice these as well. As each concept is introduced, you will want to encourage the group to engage in these each week that follows.

Group Discussion: At times there will be a question or series of questions aimed at the entire group for discussion together. These will be designated with the heading "Group Discussion"; feel free to adapt to your group.

Prayer: Pray for your group by name each week. Consider creating a GroupMe, private Facebook group, or form another way to stay connected throughout the week to encourage one another and for prayer requests. NOTE: Say up front and continue to remind the group of the importance of confidentiality and to keep things shared in group within the group only so members will be comfortable opening up with one another.

Pace of the Study: This is designed to be a twelve-week study in a group. However, every group is unique. As you teach, don't focus mainly on getting through the material each week but on helping those in your group grasp and apply the truths they study. Be sensitive to the Spirit and pause when necessary.

Bible References: You will notice this curriculum is heavily based on Scripture with many passages cited. All these need to be read aloud for the group. Having people ready to read the Scripture references ahead of time or having the references written on cards to hand out for volunteers to read will involve the group more. Of course, don't ask anyone to read aloud who is uncomfortable doing so.

Deeper in the Word: Related to this, you will see in this Leader Guide a deeper discussion of vital passages of Scripture. This is for you as you lead, offering a more thorough interpretation and application of these passages. They will be set apart in a different typeface and in a box.

For Couples in Crisis: It is quite possible, even likely, that you will discover one or more couples in crisis. They have lived for years in withdrawal, unforgiveness, bitterness, or other conflict that has created deep issues. This curriculum will help most couples to work through all of these; however, there may some instances where a couple would be best served by meeting with a pastor or a Christian counselor to help them. You will be encouraged to mention this when dealing with conflict but be aware of this as you teach. Couples also need to know that seeking help from a pastor or counselor is not a sign of weakness or failure but shows a desire for a healthy marriage.

Resources Needed: All you need for this curriculum is the Leader Guide, a Participant Guide for each person (two per couple), and all participants will need their Bibles. It would be helpful to have a whiteboard, flip chart, or other means of writing down responses at times to key questions. There will be a point where all will be encouraged to take the "Love Language" quiz as noted in the study.

INTRODUCTION

LEADER: After welcoming the group and saying a prayer, read our story below. Let the group know that we aren't marriage experts but are a couple just like them. But through our love and devotion to Jesus, we recognized serious issues in our marriage. We turned to the Lord for a radical new focus that changed the trajectory of our marriage. Let the group know that this study was born from fifteen years of walking together as a couple and training scores of couples just like you.

From the Creators, John and Julie Collier

Welcome to *3-2-1 Marriage*! We are John and Julie Collier, and we are excited to embark on a journey together with you toward a deeper understanding of God's (beautiful) unique design for Christian marriage.

As a couple, we are passionate about marriage, and it is our desire for you to learn how to become one and fulfill the divine beauty God had in mind when He created marriage.

We developed and have been leading this material for many years and have witnessed the miraculous power of doing marriage God's way in so many couples. We cannot wait to share it with you, and our prayer is that as you walk through the small group Bible study, your marriage will be strengthened and realigned and will fulfill the divine purpose God has for you as a couple!

Marriage is a sacred covenant, and a new creation that reflects the very nature of God Himself. In Genesis 2:24, it says, "Therefore a man shall leave his father and his mother and hold fast to his wife, and they shall become one flesh." This spectacular yet profound mystery reveals the depth of God's heart for the intimate union between a husband and a wife: we are to become one! Husband, wife, and Holy Spirit intertwine and transform from three to one (3-2-1)! It is a glorious transformation we are invited to experience as Christ followers!

Our story as a married couple will help you see why we are so passionate about marriage and have given so much of our lives to helping married couples move toward God's design for marriage. We met in college and were married after graduating. It was a wonderful day filled with joy and hope. We expected to live "happily ever after" and were so excited about entering into marriage together.

Early on, our marriage seemed to be going smoothly—we were involved in a local church, served in leadership, were involved in small groups and each having our daily quiet times with the Lord. We did all the things normally expected of a young couple who love Jesus and want to serve the Lord. However, we soon began to realize that something was missing in our marriage.

We were both saved at a young age, raised in Christian homes, and surrounded by Christian community throughout our dating and engagement. But we struggled to walk marriage out God's way and sensed a decline in our unity over time. We eventually got to a point in which we were living in a state of withdrawal from each other.

Because we did not have the tools or understanding to become one, we had each caused a lot of pain to the other and did not know how to find our way back to where God wanted us to be as a couple. It was a time that felt very dark in our marriage, and we did not know what to do.

It was in this difficult time that we simply began to cry out to God and ask Him to save us. We began the hard but necessary journey of asking God how to do marriage His way and letting Him knock down the walls and put us back together as He originally designed for our marriage. We slowly started praying together. We started praying over and for each other.

As we laid down our own lives and expectations, we witnessed a true miracle from the Lord, and He began to teach us straight from His Word what He had in mind when He created marriage! Our spiritual lives had been disconnected, but God began to lead us by His Holy Spirit and weave us together into ONE! Holy Spirit, husband, and wife . . . becoming ONE!

Out of our story, the Lord birthed our marriage curriculum. And it has become our joy and passion to share it with others! We have now had so many wonderful years living out marriage as God designed, and we can truly tell you: marriage as God designed is spectacular! It will far surpass what you can hope, dream, or imagine!

Our prayer is that you can have a fresh start and invite God into your marriage in a way you have never experienced—whether you are in the first year of your marriage, still in your early years, or, like us, have been married thirty years or longer. God loves you so much, and He will keep knocking at the door of your marriage until you let Him in, until you lay down all of your "good plans" in exchange for

His plans—the *best* plans for your marriage! He has an unbelievable blessing in store for you and your marriage.

As you begin this journey, remember that you are not alone. The Holy Spirit is your guide, and He will give you the courage and strength to move with courage and vulnerability as you share your struggles and victories, the glorious process of becoming ONE.

We are praying over every couple as you learn and understand how to become one as in Genesis 2:24. The journey from vow to victory really means that, from the wedding day until death, you experience the beauty and mystery of becoming one. What a beautiful picture of God's faithfulness and the image of Christ and His church.

Let's begin the journey together. Victory awaits!

Why Marriage?

Read Genesis 2:24.

Have you ever thought about why God created marriage? Marriage was God's idea, after all. That means God gets to define it, and He knows what makes it work.

1. This verse is the definition of marriage.

This verse tells us that you leave everything and that every other relationship takes a back seat to marriage. That means your parents, your children, every other relationship.

Read Matthew 19:4–6.

What does Jesus say about this verse in the New Testament? Jesus quoted this verse from Genesis and took it even further. Jesus looks back to creation and God's intent in forming man and woman and in establishing marriage.

2. God created marriage for His _glory_ and our _good_.

Read Genesis 2:15–25.

What are ways this entire passage shows us the priority of marriage to God? The first marriage in the garden was the most beautiful wedding setting in history. Sorry, folks, but your wedding may have been in an incredible venue, but it doesn't compare to paradise made by God Himself. The garden of Eden was a paradise with its beautiful surroundings, with the perfect relationship in intimacy Adam had with Eve and both had with God.

3. As beautiful as Eden was, what made it such a paradise was the unhindered _intimacy_ that Adam and Eve had with God and with one another.

We live in a consumer-driven world that gives too much focus to surface things like how nice a home is or your beautiful landscaping. Here's the truth: it doesn't matter whether you live in a beautiful garden or in a shack, when you have intimacy with God and with one another, you will be extremely fulfilled. Adam and Eve had that.

Our hearts yearn for that to this day. St. Augustine said a prayer we can all relate to: "You have made us for yourself, and our heart is restless until it finds rest in you."[1] We're made in the image of God, and our hearts are still yearning for that perfect intimacy with God and that intimacy with one another.

---

[1]   Saint Augustine, *Saint Augustine's Confessions*, trans. Henry Chadwick (New York: Oxford University Press, 2009), 3.

If marriage is so important to God, why is marriage sometimes so hard?

Read Genesis 3:1–15.

4. _Sin_ came and brought brokenness into every relationship.

We see, beginning with Adam and Eve, that marriages aren't perfect, and ours will not be. Theologians call this the _fall_. But God who is full of mercy and grace did not leave us in our sin. He lovingly made a way for us to experience new life and a relationship with Him through faith in His Son Jesus.

How can we see the promise of the good news in Jesus in Genesis 3:15?

Although brokenness extends to every relationship, including marriage, Christ also redeemed the marriage covenant. We see the New Testament describe Christ's relationship with the church, Jesus being the groom and the church being the bride.

Let's look at Jesus and His role as husband. He is our role model, men. He is our role model to show us how we're to love our wives. He's our role model for how we live our lives. Jesus loved His bride so much He laid down His life for her. Are we loving our bride that same way?

We will have weaknesses; we are self-centered and married to another self-centered person. We all carry baggage into our marriages. We all carry pain into our marriages. We all fall short. We all need mercy. But also remember that marriage is a covenant, which means the person you're married to is the person God wants you to be with.

Our Hope for You in This Study

The Christian marriage should be the most fulfilling, the most successful, and the most honored relationship. It is second only to our personal relationship with God through Jesus Christ. We have Christ as our leader and guide in our marriage. We can look at Him and see how we're supposed to live our lives and how we're supposed to live in our marriage. For us to have the intimacy and joy available to us will require intentionality, faith, and prayer. We won't drift into it; we have to be intentional.

As you walk through this study together as a couple, you will have to make a daily decision to shut the door on the world and what the world is saying about relationships because its advice is broken. Devote yourselves to do it God's way. Yes, it can be more difficult for us to do it His way because of how confused and corrupt the world's view is on relationships today. But you can be sure that God will give us the strength and the power to do it through His Spirit.

Today, as a couple, you can begin a new journey in your marriage with a renewed focus on the Lord and His purposes in marriage.

You will be learning some specific practices to help you to become more like Christ in your marriage. These include praying together daily, a weekly conversation we call a "Starbucks moment," and learning to communicate so that when you have conflict—and you will—you can move from withdrawal to intimacy.

> **LEADER:** Have 3 x 5-inch cards or paper for this discussion. Tell the group to respond anonymously and openly. Then, take up the responses. As you review these later, you can use the responses to begin praying for the group.

Without including your name, write down a brief answer to each of these questions.

1. What do you hope to learn personally from this study?
2. What is a specific area where you want to see growth in your marriage?
3. How ready are you to learn, to grow, and to be changed?

LEADER: You may want to conclude the first week by casting a vision like this:

Imagine for just a minute what it could look like if across churches in America we saw marriage after marriage displaying the presence of God in how couples love one another, their children, and above all their Lord Jesus. These are not perfect marriages, but everywhere you turn in this community or that you see couples obviously in love, praying for one another, loving their neighbors, living with joy in their daily lives. If that were true, you and I would walk in a totally different America than we see right now.

BUILDING A FOUNDATION FOR MARRIAGE, PART 1

Matthew 7:24–29

P.L.E.A.S.E.—The Keys to Building a Firm Foundation in Your Marriage

Structures not built on a firm foundation will fail the test of time. Eventually, they will crumble to the ground. That is why you must decide for yourself what foundation you will build your marriage on. Will it be God and His ways, or you and your ways? What beliefs, habits, and expectations do you bring with you as you begin this building process, and how do these affect your marital foundation?

> **LEADER—ILLUSTRATION:** If you've ever been in a city where a foundation is being laid for a skyscraper, you will notice the first thing the builders do is to drive piles of steel deep into the ground. The higher the building, the deeper the metal must go. Any structure is only as sound as its foundation.

It is crucial that you know and believe wholeheartedly what truly brings life and vitality to your relationship from the very beginning.

Once your foundation has been established, you can begin building upon it. However, you must ensure that every brick you lay is in line with the foundation of God's Word. This takes faith, prayer, work, and intentionality. Remember, your wedding ceremony is your starting point, not the finish line. You will need to continually invest prayer, faith, time, effort, knowledge, and emotional energy into your spouse/marriage in order to grow together upon the foundation you are building for your marriage.

Without an intentional pursuit of God and building our marriage on Him, we simply drift downstream with culture and suddenly find we are on an unstable foundation.

GROUP DISCUSSION

Read Matthew 7:24–29.

LEADER

Deeper in the Word

Matthew 7:24–29

Background

Jesus brings the Sermon on the Mount (Matthew 5–7) to a noteworthy climax with the comparison of two builders. In the larger concluding section of the Sermon on the Mount (Matthew 7:13–27), Jesus contrasts the two groups of people who exist—those who are disciples and those who aren't—with three illustrations:

- The narrow and broad way (7:13–14).
- Good and bad fruit (7:15–23).
- A home (that is, life) built on a rock rather than sand (7:24–27).

Jesus calls disciples to "build a solid foundation that combines authentic commitment to Christ with persevering obedience."[2]

Jesus illustrates the point with a parable that would be understood by his audience. Floods in Israel would wash away a house on sand. "From picturing two ways and two trees, our Lord closed His message by picturing two builders and their houses. The two ways illustrate the start of the life of faith; the two trees illustrate the growth and results of the life of faith here and now; and the two houses illustrate the end of this life of faith, when God shall call everything to judgment."[3]

However, Richards argues there are in fact four examples: "two ways (vv. 13–14), two trees (vv. 15–20), two claims (vv. 21–23), and two builders (vv. 24–27)."[4]

Supporting passages: Luke 6:48 (parallel); Matthew 5:17–48 (v. 19); James 1:22–25 (doer of the word, v. 24 here).

Investigation

Verse 24: "Everyone then who hears these words of mine." "The possessive pronoun mine is in the emphatic beginning

---

2   Craig Blomberg, *Matthew*, The New American Commentary, vol. 22 (Nashville: Broadman & Holman, 1992), 134.

3   Warren W. Wiersbe, *The Bible Exposition Commentary*, vol. 1 (Wheaton, IL: Victor Books, 1996), 31.

4   Lawrence O. Richards, *The Bible Reader's Companion*, electronic ed. (Wheaton, IL: Victor Books, 1991), 609.

position in that phrase. Jesus was equating his own words with the will of his Father (7:21). Jesus was claiming to have the same authority as the God who authored the Old Testament Scriptures—a claim he also implied in clarifying the original intent of the law in 5:17–48."[5]

"And does them." See James 1:22–25.

> But be doers of the word, and not hearers only, deceiving yourselves. For if anyone is a hearer of the word and not a doer, he is like a man who looks intently at his natural face in a mirror. For he looks at himself and goes away and at once forgets what he was like. But the one who looks into the perfect law, the law of liberty, and perseveres, being no hearer who forgets but a doer who acts, he will be blessed in his doing.

"Built." The verb is a perfect indicative passive denoting the state of completion in the past. It was built on the Rock and was impervious to the storms.

"On the rock." "The true Christian is founded on the Rock, Christ Jesus."[6]

Verse 25: "Floods came." Flash floods were common in Israel, often washing out flimsy structures. But this house was not harmed because "it had been founded on the rock." This pictures the disciple whose life is founded on Jesus, our Rock of salvation (1 Peter 2:4–5).

---

5   Stuart K. Weber, *Matthew*, Holman New Testament Commentary, vol. 1 (Nashville: Broadman & Holman, 2000), 103.

6   Wiersbe, *Bible Exposition Commentary*, 36.

Verse 26: "A foolish man who built his house on the sand." This is a direct contrast to the wise builder. There is no chance of confusing the two.

Verse 27: "Great was the fall of it." Both of these builders heard the words of Jesus. But the foolish builder rejected those words. "The first man was wise; the second man was foolish. The first man found stability and blessing in this life and in eternity; the second experienced calamity in this life and in eternity (the rain, floods, and winds can represent both hardships in this life and God's final judgment). Notice that wisdom (the rock) means to put the words of Jesus into practice."[7]

Verse 28: "Astonished." This comes from two words that mean "to strike out of." "They were astounded. We have a similar expression, though not so strong: 'I was struck with this or that remarkable thing.'"[8]

"At his teaching." "This union of the verb and participle emphasizes the idea of duration or habit."[9]

Verse 29: "Not as their scribes." They had heard many sermons before from rabbis in the synagogues.

Importance

The point is that one man showed wisdom in building on rock while the other was careless. Luke's account clarifies this point,

---

7   Weber, *Matthew*, 103.

8   Marvin Richardson Vincent, *Word Studies in the New Testament*, vol. 1 (New York: Charles Scribner's Sons, 1887), 51.

9   Vincent, *Word Studies in the New Testament*, 51.

as the wise man "dug deep and laid the foundation on the rock" (Luke 6:48); the foolish man simply "built a house on the ground without a foundation" (6:49).

Vincent tells a more recent example of this in that region told by John Kitto:

> At this very day the mode of building in Christ's own town of Nazareth suggests the source of this image. Dr. Robinson was entertained in the house of a Greek Arab. The house had just been built, and was not yet finished. In order to lay the foundations he had dug down to the solid rock, as is usual throughout the country here, to the depth of thirty feet, and then built up arches.[10]

Wiersbe says:

> Obedience to His will is the test of true faith in Christ. The test is not words, not saying "Lord, Lord," and not obeying His commands. How easy it is to learn a religious vocabulary, and even memorize Bible verses and religious songs, and yet not obey God's will. When a person is truly born again, he has the Spirit of God living within (Rom. 8:9); and the Spirit enables him to know and do the Father's will. God's love in his heart (Romans 5:5) motivates him to obey God and serve others.[11]

Implications

In many ways, a marriage resembles the life of any disciple who follows Jesus. Eugene Peterson notes two key terms for

---

10 Vincent, *Word Studies in the New Testament*, 51.

11 Warren W. Wiersbe, *Be Loyal: Following the King of Kings* (Colorado Springs: David C. Cook, 1980), 70.

those who follow Jesus: *disciple*, a learner, and *pilgrim*, one on a journey.[12] Believers spend their entire lives on a journey of growth, learning, and moving forward. To stand still is to be put at risk. Marriages are the same way. A Christian marriage represents two people walking together as disciples, learning from Jesus, and on a journey together to do his will.

Building a marriage on the sound foundation of God's Word is vital, but it is only the beginning. Just as a couple moves from a loft apartment to a townhouse, to a single-family home, to new additions as children come along, the marriage will be in trouble if it doesn't continue to grow. But that growth is strengthened by a sound foundation.

We need to take care here, as someone could mistake Jesus's words in the Sermon and in this passage to be declaring a works salvation: "Do these things and you are right before God, but fail to do them and you are not." This is the very thing Jesus was speaking against. He is describing what life in the kingdom is like, based on his fulfillment of the law (Matthew 5:17). Romans 3:21–26 tells us through Christ we have righteousness by faith. Jesus is describing what a disciple who walks by faith looks like and how he or she would respond to a difficult storm.

James, Jesus's half brother, possibly had this sermon in mind and the conclusion especially when he declared that the way to know someone has faith is because of their works (James 2:18).

---

12 Eugene H. Peterson, *A Long Obedience in the Same Direction: Discipleship in an Instant Society* (Downers Grove, IL: InterVarsity, 2000), 17.

If we want to build on the Rock, what must we do?

_____

_____

_____

_____

_____

How does this differ from building on sand?

_____

_____

_____

_____

You must decide what will be the foundation of your marriage. It's one of the most important decisions you will make in life and one you will need to return to again and again.

Time + Unintentionality = Failure

LEADER: You might point out that we don't drift into things that are important and healthy. We don't drift toward healthy eating; fast food and junk food alternatives are too available and cheap. We don't drift toward spiritual growth but discipline ourselves to study God's Word daily and spend time in prayer. To quote John Maxwell, "Everything worthwhile in life is uphill."[13] Being intentional in your pursuit of God's design for marriage is vital.

GROUP DISCUSSION

Read Romans 12:1–2; Deuteronomy 24:5; and Matthew 19:5.

How do these three passages help in establishing the foundation of your marriage?

_____

_____

_____

_____

_____

How important is it to be intentional as a couple?

_____

_____

_____

_____

---

13 John Maxwell, "The View from the Top of the Hill," John C. Maxwell, July 12, 2016, https://www.johnmaxwell.com/blog/the-view-from-the-top-of-the-hill.

> **LEADER:** Deuteronomy 24:5 makes it clear that laying a firm marital foundation takes time, learning, and intentionality; and Matthew 19:5 makes it clear that a healthy beginning to a marriage entails leaving your respective families to become a new one. Undergirding everything, Matthew 7:24–29 makes it clear that in order for anything we do to last, it must be rooted in obedience to the Word of God. This is crucial for your marriage and life.

Read Galatians 6:7.

Compare/contrast God's way versus cultural norms of our day.

_____

_____

_____

_____

_____

A Gospel Foundation

GROUP DISCUSSION

Read 1 Corinthians 15:1–7.

What does Paul say is of first importance for the believer?

_____

_____

_____

_____

_____

How do we apply that to our marriage?

_____

_____

_____

_____

_____

LEADER: Marriage is the most important and serious relationship you can have in this life. But there is a relationship that matters more and that plays the critical role in a marriage that follows God's blueprint. That is the relationship we have with God through the good news (the gospel) of Jesus Christ.

Paul says the gospel is of FIRST IMPORTANCE. When a husband and wife each receive the gospel by faith, each is in a relationship with God that can give both encouragement and wisdom for marriage.

The gospel is costly: it cost the very death of Jesus (1 Corinthians 15:3). The gospel is God's plan for humanity throughout all the Bible (note that "in accordance with the Scriptures" is stated twice in this passage). God's plan for our salvation is the gift of salvation received by grace through faith (Ephesians 2:8–9). God's plan for marriage is built on the foundation of that good news. As God forgave us our sins, husbands and wives must exercise forgiveness toward one another. As God gives us grace (that which we don't deserve) and mercy (holding back judgment we do deserve), so couples show grace and mercy to one another.

P.L.E.A.S.E.

The P.L.E.A.S.E. acronym is designed to highlight fundamental elements of biblical marriage. Taking the time to grasp these ideas and intentionally and apply them to your marriage will assist you in laying a firm foundation.

P Is for Prayer

1. **Pray** together daily: Invite God to be in the center/guide in the building blocks of your relationship. There is nothing more important for your marriage than daily prayer together as a couple. If you aren't doing this, start today. Don't worry if it seems awkward or if it hasn't been a practice you share, just get started.

From John

Be yourself when you pray together. When I pray, it's simple and to the point. When Julie prays, it's beautiful, like a poem, descriptive and lovely; you could write them down and put them in a book. Doesn't matter. God cares about prayer from the heart. So be yourself. God just wants your heart to invite Him into your marriage.

From Julie

Don't be critical of your husband's prayers. His prayer will look and sound different than yours. That is OK! Don't correct him. Be thankful and know that God is at work in all of our prayers.

LEADER: Be very encouraging here. Couples who have not been praying together may feel guilty or feel awkward about starting. This is not a time to condemn but to lift up. Let them know it's OK to find it awkward or challenging at first but to keep working together to find a daily time and place to pray as a couple.

---

2. The most intimate act between a man and a woman is _praying together_ . Your goal is to develop spiritual intimacy in your marriage (Matthew 7:7–8; Matthew 18:19–20; 1 John 5:14–15).

It is important to know the divorce rate for Christian spouses who pray together is less than 1 percent, while those who do not pray together have a divorce rate of approximately 50 percent.[14] Praying couples are also happier, more satisfied with their marriages, and less prone to conflict.

GROUP DISCUSSION

Read Matthew 7:7–8; Matthew 18:19–20; and 1 John 5:14–15.

How do these verses motivate spouses to pray together?

_____

_____

---

14 Donald R. Downing, *Marriage from the Heart: A Revolutionary Approach to Covenant Marriage* (Maitland, FL: Xulon, 2010), 75.

_____

_____

_____

Practically, how might prayer together look in a marriage?

_____

_____

_____

_____

What hinders couples from praying together?

_____

_____

_____

_____

Discuss how praying together increases spiritual, emotional, and physical intimacy.

LEADER: Spiritual intimacy will lead to emotional intimacy, which leads to physical intimacy. You can remind the group here of Adam and Eve. God created them and us to be known and loved. In the garden of Eden, they were naked and had no shame. They were physically transparent, and they were emotionally, physically, and spiritually intimate.

What was the first thing that they did after they sinned? They covered themselves and they hid. They were no longer physically, emotionally, or spiritually intimate. That's what sin does. Sin covers us with fear, guilt, and shame. It shatters intimacy.

But through Christ, we can once again have spiritual intimacy with God and each other. Your spiritual intimacy will lead to greater emotional intimacy, which is going to lead into greater physical intimacy. This is why prayer is so vital. Statistics show only 8 percent of Christian spouses pray together.[15] This is confusing since studies have proven the success or failure of marriage can be related to praying together. Couples who pray together daily are happier, more intimate, more satisfied, and have less conflict.

Let prayer be a first response and not a last resort. For example:

> **Example A:** Bill and Sally have been praying together since they got married. They try to pray for one another throughout the day, but they also set aside time each day to pray with each other. They aren't perfect spouses, but the more they realize their imperfections, the more they are driven to their knees. As they ask God for help to love one another better, He shows each of them areas in which they are acting selfishly. He then draws them to depend on Him for greater measures of Christlike love, and with each passing day—by God's

---

15 Dennis Rainey, "Prayer: The Secret to a Lasting Marriage," Crosswalk, September 10, 2005, https://www.crosswalk.com/family/marriage/prayer-the -secret-to-a-lasting-marriage-1173307.html.

grace—they are learning to love each other more and more selflessly.

Example B: Jack and Mary, on the other hand, offer up a hurried blessing before each meal, pray a little bit on their own, but never pray together. It's not that they meant to leave that out, they just always figure there will be time to do it later—and later never comes. Over time, they grow continually more irritated with one another over little things, grow bitter, and quietly begin to drift apart. One day, after a huge argument, they realize just how bad things have gotten. They decide to ask God for help to restore their marriage, but with all the wounds they've inflicted on each other, there's little doubt that the road to healing will be a long and painful one.

How do these testimonials encourage you to pray together to build spiritual intimacy?

_____

_____

_____

_____

_____

_____

**3. Continue to invest in one another through intentional acts of
  love .** It's important that we define love according to God's Word as a building block in your marriage (1 John 4:7–8; Colossians 3:12–15; and 1 Corinthians 13:4–7).

L Is for Love

GROUP DISCUSSION

Read Romans 5:6–8.

How does this explain God's love for us?

_____

_____

_____

_____

_____

God who is holy and perfect loves us unconditionally in spite of our imperfections. Is love measured by the character of the one giving or receiving?

_____

_____

_____

_____

4. List at least three things your spouse does that make you feel loved.

_____

_____

_____

_____

_____

Did any spouses share the same answers? Do we have a tendency to love our spouse as we desire to be loved? "Love is not love unless it is received by the one being loved."

Read Ephesians 5:25–29, 33; and 1 Peter 3:1–2.

Discuss how husband and wife are to love each other.

_____

_____

_____

_____

_____

Example: While dating/engaged, Billy and Sally talked very much during dates and through texts, phone calls, and messages. This made Sally feel very loved by Billy, and she couldn't wait until their marriage so she could be with Billy all the time. She envisioned late nights talking and deep conversations every day as when they were dating. Billy loved talking with Sally. She was always so respectful of him and complimented him often. She would cook for him and take him meals when he was working late. After the marriage, he envisioned Sally cooking for him often, and building him up with her words and presence. However, once the wedding was over, Billy came home from work tired and often did not want to talk about his long day. He would often want to watch the game or a movie. Sally, also tired from her day, would not want to cook for Billy but would just want to go out. Billy wondered, *What happened to the happy cook who always built me up?* and Sally wondered, *Where is my once talkative Billy?* How will they make sense of this change in their relationship?

When does love for your spouse become an action/decision versus an emotion?

_____

_____

_____

_____

_____

5. Our love for __God__ should motivate us to love/respect our spouses unconditionally (1 John 5:3).

6. God's love for _us_ shows us how much He loves us so we can love each other well (Romans 5:8).

When is it most difficult to love our spouses?

_____

_____

_____

_____

_____

Do we have a plan for loving/respecting them when they do not deserve it?

_____

_____

_____

_____

_____

The answer to that question will determine the type of marriage you will have. Do you desire a marriage built on the sand—or the Rock? (Proverbs 3:5–6; Matthew 7:24–29)

7. Remember: _pray_ first and ask the Lord to help you. He is faithful even when we aren't. He gave you the wonderful gift of marriage, and He created you to be an instrument of agape love to your spouse. When you love God, you will love one another. What will be your foundation? (Psalm 127:1; Matthew 7:7–8)

A man full of the Spirit of God will love his wife "as Christ loved the church and gave himself up for her" (Ephesians 5:25). A woman full of the Spirit will respect her husband "as to the Lord" (Ephesians 5:22). As a result, they will both bring one another closer to the Lord through their marriage and point a lost world to Christ (Romans 8:9).

A Practical Aid: The "Starbucks Moment"

By "Starbucks moment," we mean a weekly time you get together as a couple to talk about things that are vital in your marriage. For you it may be a "Chick-fil-A moment," a "let's go for a walk moment," or something else that fits. The key is to have these regular meetings to talk about life and your marriage **and to do so when you are not tired, stressed, or hurt**. If this is not a regular part of your marriage you can start now and include discussing things you are learning in this study.

> **LEADER:** Here is where to note there will be a few specific and very practical practices couples will want to engage in. The two most important are praying together daily and the "Starbucks moment" described here. It's most important that couples begin praying together daily but encourage them to pursue a weekly "Starbucks moment" (or whatever you want to call it that fits your community) within the first few weeks. The discussion below could be the first instance of this for the couples as they consider these questions together.

> **LEADER:** The following can be completed by the couples before the next lesson. Please be sure to encourage them to take the "Love Languages" quiz online as noted. Be sure to do so as well. You could begin next week's lesson with a few people sharing what they learned.

NOTE: This week each of you will need to take a few minutes and take the "Love Languages" quiz at https://5lovelanguages.com/. This is an excellent way to help establish a baseline for understanding how to love and serve one another more effectively.

Review and Application

1. What kind of marriage do you both desire?

_____

_____

_____

_____

2. What are the building blocks of your marriage going to be?

_____

_____

_____

_____

3. Do you both agree to trust God and His way? What does that mean for each of you individually? Do you both have to be intentional?

_____

_____

_____

_____

4. Do you both desire to grow in being one spiritually? If so, do you commit to pray together daily? Discuss the importance of unity in marriage, and how to build unity apart from God—is that possible?

_____

_____

_____

_____

_____

5. How do you both see love? Does your spouse know? How can you communicate your love language to one another? Do you have to be intentional?

_____

_____

_____

_____

_____

BUILDING A FOUNDATION FOR MARRIAGE, PART 2

Matthew 7:24–29

> **LEADER:** Briefly review the previous week's points as noted below and consider asking anyone to share with the group something helpful they've learned so far.

P.L.E.A.S.E.—The Keys to Building a God-Centered Foundation (*continued*)

Review Matthew 7:24–29. If we want to build on the Rock, what must we do? How does this differ from building on sand? You must decide what will be the foundation of your marriage.

P stands for _prayer_ .

L stands for _love_ .

> Remember: Time + Unintentionality = Failure

Marriage is a gift from God, and we have seen that living out our marriage according to His ways is our gift back to Him. *If you are newlyweds, you are building the foundation of your marriage.* If you have been married for some time, you can strengthen or, if necessary, rebuild your foundation. Wherever you are in your marital journey, God is for you! Reviewing the foundation of marriage is an ever-vital need.

Whether you realize it or not, your marriage is based on something. Will you live your marriage based on the Word of God or something else? It is very important to learn, begin, and continue habits in your relationship that are consistent with God's word that will bring life, vitality, and intimacy to your marriage. Let's talk about what God's word says about marriage, and what you can do to make sure your marriage is based on the Rock? What is the Rock? (2 Timothy 3:16–17; Romans 12:1–2)

GROUP DISCUSSION

Read Genesis 2:18; 1 Peter 3:7; Malachi 2:13–16.

How do these verses show how your marriage affects your relationship with God?

_____

_____

_____

_____

_____

_____

Has society abandoned a God-centered marriage? What has been the impact of this?

_____

_____

_____

_____

_____

1. **The first two building blocks that should be present in a Christian marriage are __prayer__ together and __love__** (Genesis 25:21; 1 John 4:19; Ephesians 5:25, 33).

2. **Note: love is spelled " __respect__ " to the husband.**

E Is for Evangelize

3. **We are commanded to __evangelize__ our spouse** (Ephesians 5:25–27; 1 Peter 3:1–2).

> **LEADER:** Evangelism literally means to tell the good news of Jesus Christ. The word comes from two words in the Greek language: *eu*, which means "good" (as in euphoria!), and *angel* or "message." It literally means to tell the good news about Jesus's work on the cross for our salvation, and that is the best of good news!

Our words *gospel* and *evangelism* in the New Testament are actually the same word: *euangelizo*. We see evangelism practiced when believers tell unbelievers the good news so they can receive forgiveness and become followers of Jesus.

There's another way to think of the gospel, or good news, that relates to believers who've received salvation. Salvation is the beginning of a journey made possible by good news, but the same good news also guides us on the journey as we grow throughout our lives.

But even as we have experienced salvation, we still get pulled back to self-righteousness. That's why Paul kept reminding believers in his epistles to keep focused on the gospel. We have to keep evangelizing ourselves or as some put it, we keep preaching the gospel to ourselves.

Christian couples evangelize each other as we remind each other of the truth of the gospel. If Jesus's work on the cross and resurrection can save us for all eternity, He can also help us in the daily issues we face in our marriage, and that's good news!

After reading Ephesians 5:25–27 and 1 Peter 3:1–2, what does *evangelize* mean to you? Do you see your marriage as a mission field opportunity?

_____

_____

_____

_____

_____

> **LEADER:** Explain that the passage in 1 Peter 3:1–2 is specifically addressing a woman whose husband is not a believer, showing that the way to reach him is not to nag him to Jesus but to demonstrate a changed life. But we can apply this to believers who are married in that the best way to encourage one another to grow in Jesus is not for one spouse to preach at the other, but by humbly showing the truth of salvation by one's life.

How do we live out these verses? (*Hint:* John 14:15–16)

_____

_____

_____

_____

_____

We have a tendency to love only when we feel loved. However, this is not how God loves us. He has called you as His children to take upon His nature to love as He loves. God's love is *agape* love, which in Greek is translated as unconditional and sacrificial. This means the husband loves his wife even when he feels disrespected. This also means the wife respects her husband even when she feels unloved.

When we as a married couple choose to love unconditionally when we feel unloved or disrespected, we bring our spouse to the Lord. God designed the marriage covenant to be a sanctifying relationship when we agree to love God first and most and then love our spouse unconditionally as Ephesians 5:25–27 says.

LEADER: Here is a story that's optional but one that gives a powerful example. While it describes an unbelieving husband coming to Christ, it can also demonstrate how to live out the gospel as a married couple.

British Baptist pastor Charles Spurgeon lived in the 1800s. In a sermon he told this amazing story, which illustrates 1 Peter 3:1–2:

[A] husband who was a . . . depraved man of the world . . . had a wife who for many years bore with his ridicule and unkindness, praying for him day and night, though no change came over him, except that he grew even more bold in sin. One night, being at a drunken feast with a number of his boon companions, he boasted that his wife would do anything he wished, she was as submissive as a lamb. "Now," he said, "she has gone to bed hours ago; but if I take you all to my house at once she will get up and entertain you and make no complaint." "Not she," they said, and the matter ended in a bet, and away they went. It was in the small hours of the night, but in a few minutes she was up, and remarked that she was glad that she had two chickens ready, and if they would wait a little she would soon have a supper spread for them. They waited, and ere long, at that late hour, the table was spread, and she took her place at it as if it was quite an ordinary matter, acting the part of hostess with cheerfulness. One of the company, touched in his better feelings, exclaimed, "Madam, we ought to apologize to you for intruding upon you in this way, and at such an hour, but I am at a loss to understand how it is you receive us so cheerfully, for being a religious person you cannot approve of our conduct." Her reply was, "I and my husband were both formerly unconverted, but, by the grace of God, I am now a believer in the Lord Jesus. I have daily prayed for my husband, and

I have done all I can to bring him to a better mind, but as I see no charge in him, I fear he will be lost for ever; and I have made up my mind to make him as happy as I can while he is here." They went away, and her husband said, "Do you really think I shall be unhappy for ever?" "I fear so," said she, "I would to God you would repent and seek forgiveness." That night patience accomplished her desire. He was soon found with her on the way to heaven![16]

A Is for Ask

4. We should continue to _ask_: "How can I make you feel more loved?" (Matthew 19:5–6; Philippians 2:3–8).

Continue the things you did when you were dating/engaged that made you want to get married in the first place: humility, perseverance, love. Your marriage is not defined by a few big moments but rather in the small day-to-day moments of prayer, love, mercy, grace, and forgiveness given freely to one another consistent with God's word.

Marriage is a life of humility, service, and teamwork. It's the gift you give that keeps on giving—to you! What degree of expertise do you have with your spouse? Do you know what makes them feel love from you? Our love for God and our walk as a follower of Christ has everything to do with our marriage. Love God first, then you are able to love your spouse.

---

16 Charles Spurgeon, "A Word for the Persecuted" (sermon 1188, Metropolitan Tabernacle, London, August 16, 1874), https://ccel.org/ccel/spurgeon/sermons 20/sermons20.v_1.html.

```
                    GOD
                    /\
                   /  \
                  /    \
                 /      \
                /        \
               /          \
              / FOUNDATION \
             /   Matthew     \
            /   7:24–27        \
           /                    \
   YOU    /_____\   SPOUSE
```

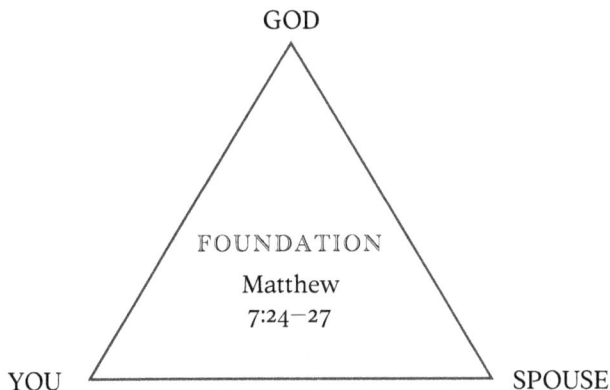

What will be the foundation of your marriage?

LEADER: Explain how the foundation of marriage is God's Word as we saw in Matthew 7:24–27. As each spouse, grounded on the Word, pursues God with all their heart, he or she will be drawn closer to one another as they draw closer to God, just as moving up each side of the triangle illustrates.

LEADER—BONUS MATERIAL: Here is a place where you as a leader could give practical advice from your own experience, or you might give the following (not in the participant guide) as a possible goal for their marriages:

In addition to regular "Starbucks moments," these three commitments have helped many marriages through the years:

1. *Dialogue Daily:* Take time to talk and hear one another daily and include praying together as the most vital part of this.

> 2. *Date Weekly:* Have one night where phones are off and where you focus on each other. It can be a stay-at-home movie night or going out to eat, whatever you want. It reminds you both how important couple time is. The "Starbucks moment" could be a part of date night.
>
> 3. *Depart Quarterly:* Put at least a quarterly overnight getaway in your budget. Your marriage is worth it!

Review and Application

Read Romans 12:1–2.

LEADER

Deeper in the Word

Romans 12:1–2

Background

How do we respond to the gospel? Once we have experienced the mercy and grace through faith in Jesus Christ, how are we to live? In Romans 12:1–2, Paul begins to explain this in detail, basing it on previous chapters, Romans 1–11. After giving a comprehensive theological discussion on salvation through Jesus Christ (Romans 1–8) and the application of salvation to Jews (Romans 9–11), Paul turns to practical matters. This passage is the hinge that swings open the door from doctrinal truth to practical application.

In Romans, we see the grand narrative of Scripture laid out in one epistle:

- **Creation** (Romans 1:20).
- **Fall** and the misery of sin (1:18–3:20).
- **Redemption** through Jesus Christ (3:21–11:36).
- **Restoration** to a relationship with and service to God (12:1–16:27) and the hope of the restoration of all things (Romans 8:31–39).

In Romans 12:1–2, then we see that the "believer's response to God's mercy is personal sacrifice that will strengthen life in the church as well as personal relationships."[17]

Supporting passages: Romans 6:1–14; Ephesians 4:1–6; and Colossians 3:1–11.

Investigation

Verse 1: This single verse is perhaps more pregnant with truth than any other single verse in the Bible.

"Therefore." Paul is saying that Christian practice (Romans 12–16) is founded on Christian doctrine (1–11). It is also central to our worship, as verse 1 indicates here.

The "therefore" in verse 1 relates to Romans 1–11: "It marks the transition from the theology of God's redemptive act in Christ Jesus to the ethical expectations that flow logically from that theological base."[18]

We do what God says in daily life because of what we know and experience through salvation in Jesus: "Only the

---

17 Kenneth Boa and William Kruidenier, *Romans*, Holman New Testament Commentary, vol. 6 (Nashville: Broadman & Holman, 2000), 361.

18 Robert H. Mounce, *Romans*, The New American Commentary, vol. 27 (Nashville: Broadman & Holman, 1995), 230.

Christian faith, rooted as it is in a supernatural act that took place in history (the incarnation, life, death, and resurrection of Jesus Christ), has the ultimate moral authority as well as the effective power to transform human life according to the divine intention. So Christian ethics are practical specifically because they do not stand alone but emerge as unavoidable implications of an established theological base."[19]

"I appeal to you." Literally, "I call you alongside me." The Greek term is from *parakaleo*, which Jesus used to speak of the Holy Spirit, the Comforter or Helper in John 14:16, 26. It can be translated as "I exhort," a strong appeal to believers. Chapters 1–11 focus on exposition or explaining the riches of salvation in Christ, while chapters 12–16 exhort believers to live out their faith based on chapters 1–11.

"Brothers." Inclusive of brothers and sisters, clearly directed to the church.

"By the mercies of God." *Mercy* is the undeserved kindness in which God withholds our deserved judgment because of Christ. This phrase summarizes all of Romans chapters 1–11. Used in other verses including these (with the English translation of the term italicized):

"So if there is any encouragement in Christ, any comfort from love, any participation in the Spirit, any affection and *sympathy*" (Philippians 2:1, author's emphasis).

---

19 Mounce, *Romans*, 230.

"Put on then, as God's chosen ones, holy and beloved, *compassionate* hearts, kindness, humility, meekness, and patience" (Colossians 3:12, author's emphasis).

"Present your bodies." *Present* is a technical term related to Levitical sacrifices and means "present once for all." *Bodies* includes our physical bodies but also represents the totality of who we are: "Just as Jesus Christ had to take on Himself a body in order to accomplish God's will on earth, so we must yield our bodies to Christ that He might continue God's work through us."[20]

"God's mercy resulted in our being bought out of the slave market of sin and adopted into the household of righteousness. Therefore, our **bodies** are to become **living sacrifices** as we **worship** the one who redeemed us by his **mercy**."[21]

"A living sacrifice, holy and acceptable." Note *living* sacrifice rather than the sacrifices slain in the Old Testament. We are to continually die to self and live to Christ. The metaphor looks back to the sacrificial system. New Testament scholar F. F. Bruce comments that "the sacrifices of the new order do not consist in taking the lives of others, like the ancient animal sacrifices, but in giving one's own."[22]

Holy denotes the sacrifice is set apart for God. Our sacrifice must be *living* to reflect the total surrender to the Lord; it must be

---

20 Warren W. Wiersbe, *The Bible Exposition Commentary*, vol. 1 (Wheaton, IL: Victor Books, 1996), 554. See Romans 6:11–14 and Philippians 1:20 where Paul also uses the body to refer to the totality of a person.

21 Boa and Kruidenier, *Romans*, 363–64.

22 "Romans 12:1 Commentary," Precept Austin, November 23, 2022, https://www .preceptaustin.org/romans_12_word_studies.

holy because the Holy Spirit lives within us and God is holy and *acceptable* because God graciously receives such a surrendered life of His children.

"Spiritual worship" The word *spiritual* is literally "logic," or reasonable. But in this context, it could also refer to being spiritual in the sense that the worship being expressed is true or correct. *Worship* is the term *latreia*, which was a common term for priestly duties in the temple. We no longer go to a temple because we are the temple of the Holy Spirit (1 Corinthians 6:19).

Dallas Willard noted that grace is opposed to *earning*, but not to *effort*. We are redeemed only by God's grace, but we willfully choose to surrender our lives to Him as a living sacrifice, which pleases Him! We no longer have to make a sacrifice—Jesus did that! We only offer ourselves as living sacrifices.

Verse 2: Verse 1 tells us to present ourselves to God as a living sacrifice; verse 2 tells us two ways (one negative, the next positive) to carry out this in our lives. Paul gives the goal in verse 1 and how to live it in verse 2.

"Do not be conformed to this world." *Conformed* comes from a word from which we get the word *scheme* as in "a pattern." We are no longer partakers in the scheme set up in our fallen world. The idea here is STOP being conformed. *World* means the age in which we live and includes "the beliefs, the philosophies, the methodologies, and the strategies of the fallen world in which we live. It is not just the world and its people in their fallen state. It is the worldviews and practices that derive from the fallen state that define the age in which humans live at any time in history."[23]

J. B. Phillips's translation, "don't let the world around you squeeze you into its own mould," helps show the intent of these words. This shows the stark difference between being conformed to this world system and being a citizen of heaven:

> As citizens of heaven (Phil 3:20) we are to "set [our] minds on things above, not on earthly things" (Col 3:2). Paul reminded the Galatians that the present age is evil (Gal 1:4). It cannot, and must not, serve as a model for Christian living. Its values and goals are antithetical to growth in holiness. The church should stand out from the world as a demonstration of God's intention for the human race. To be culturally identified with the world is to place the church at risk. Believers are to be salt and light (Matt 5:13–14), purifying and enlightening contemporary culture.[24]

Conformity to this world is *unbecoming* of a Christian: we were made for different! Conformity to this world is *unhelpful* for a Christian: the world will not deliver what it promises.

"But be transformed." We get our word *metamorphosis* from this Greek term. It is also used of Jesus's transfiguration in Matthew 17:2. This means a change of form, or a real, obvious, deep change that happens in conversion. The verb is *continuous*: we are to continue to grow as long as we have breath. There are always next steps to take for the believer in our transformative journey. We never arrive in this life (Philippians 3:12–14). It is in

---

23 Boa and Kruidenier, *Romans*, 364–65.
24 Mounce, *Romans*, 232.

the passive voice, which means "let yourself be transformed." As Paul staked out in Romans 8, this is the work of the Spirit in progressive sanctification as we are continually conformed more to the image of Jesus (Romans 8:26–29). It is an imperative, a command, not an option.

"By the renewal of your mind." Note first that our emotions or feelings are not the point. Today people tend to think something is real when they feel a certain way; in Scripture, we do God's will, and the feelings follow after our obedience. *Renewing* comes from two Greek words meaning "new" and "again," used of renewal or revival. Paul used the term in 2 Corinthians 4:16: "our inner self is being renewed day by day." We do this through the consistent study and application of the Word (Psalm 1), worshipping, and trusting God in the circumstances of life.

"You may discern." This word was used by Greeks to describe the testing of metals by fire to show the genuineness of coins. It can mean both to test something's validity and to prove value. A renewed mind is the one that can understand God's will.

"Good and acceptable and perfect." Paul offers a triad of terms to describe the unique nature of God's will. It is always good. It is always the most acceptable way to live. And it is perfect. Nothing we experience in this life compares to walking in the will of God.

"Will of God." The way to know the will of God is to do the will of God: as we present our whole lives to God daily, turning from the world system to be continually changed by our renewed minds, we will come to know more clearly God's will. And when it is not clear, we can trust Him to guide us.

Importance

These verses frame the Christian life: we received God's mercy in salvation (justification), and now we continually turn from the world and are being transformed (sanctification). As the triangle illustration shows, marriages should be built on the Rock that is Jesus (Matthew 7:24–27, Week 1). Marriages grow following Romans 12:1–2: as the husband and wife pursue Jesus, they are drawn closer both to Him and to one another.

Wiersbe shows the importance of the passage to marriage in his description of the word *present*: "It commands a definite commitment of the body to the Lord, just as a bride and groom in their wedding service commit themselves to each other. It is this once-for-all commitment that determines what they do with their bodies."[25] The passage tells us to give our *bodies* to God (v. 1), to give our *minds* to God, and our *wills* to God (v. 2). Married couples do the same: first to Jesus but also to one another. We give our whole selves to one another, including our bodies (1 Corinthians 7:4–5).

Implications

God loves us too much to let us stay where we are, so He calls us to continually be presenting ourselves as living sacrifices, forsaking the world, and becoming more like Christ.

We don't drift into this; we must renew our minds constantly, push ourselves consistently to think more and be more like Jesus. But this is not based on our willpower or ability but on

---

25 Warren W. Wiersbe, *Be Right: How to Be Right with God, Yourself, and Others* (Colorado Springs: David C. Cook, 1977), 148–49.

the Spirit's work within us (Romans 8). What God calls us to do is not always easy; marriage has its challenges! But God equips and empowers His children to do His will. As spouses seek to know the Lord more through His Word (12:2), are stirred to worship by presenting themselves living sacrifices to God (12:1), and walk in ways that follow God's best and not the world (12:2; also Psalm 1), they both grow closer to God and one another.

1. What are ways you can apply Romans 12:1–2 to your marriage?

_____

_____

_____

_____

_____

2. As we have discussed so far, the foundation of a godly marriage includes *prayer*, *love*, *evangelize*, and *ask*. After reading Ephesians 5:25–27 and 1 Peter 3:1–2, do you see the God-given power you possess in the life of your spouse? Are you acting as a light pointing your spouse to the Lord?

_____

_____

_____

_____

_____

3. Knowing the unconditional love of the husband leads his wife to holiness, should the husband be motivated to love his wife?

_____

_____

_____

_____

_____

4. Knowing the unconditional respect of the wife leads her husband to the Lord, should she be motivated to respect him?

_____

_____

_____

_____

_____

5. How has praying together the past couple of weeks changed your relationship?

_____

_____

_____

_____

_____

Through the unconditional love of the husband and the unconditional respect of the wife in the Christian marriage, the marriage is "God centered" and points a lost world to Christ Himself.

Husbands—pray and ask the Lord to help you love your wife unconditionally. Have a plan for loving her when she does not deserve it.

Wives—pray and ask the Lord to help you respect your husband unconditionally. Have a plan for respecting him when he does not deserve it.

Together, discuss what you both agree will be the foundation of your marriage—The Word of God (the Rock) or something else (the sand). Ask God to help you, and He will!

You are building the foundation of your marriage on something whether you are intentional or not. As you learn the biblical foundation of marriage, you will have to "live it out" intentionally.

BUILDING A FOUNDATION
FOR MARRIAGE, PART 3

Matthew 7:24–29

Will you build your marriage on the Rock? (Matthew 7:24–27)

God gave us His Word to bless us and show us how to live. But He also gives us the freedom to accept or reject His Word. This verse discusses the difference between those who hear and obey, in contrast with those who only hear. It is a blessing to know that if we follow His Word, He is faithful to hold us, protect us, and bless us as His children.

Thank you, Lord! Our love for our heavenly Father is measured through obedience (2 Timothy 3:16–17; John 14:21, 23; Ephesians 5:15–17).

In Ephesians 5:16, Paul tells us to make the best use of our time. The New Testament has two words for time. One is *chronos* and means time like on a calendar or our watch, and the other means time as in the significance of the time, as in an important season.

That word, *kairos*, is what Paul uses here. As we review our lives, we can see seasons of life: some are like spring, full of promise and joy; some may be like winter, harsher and more difficult. Marriages have seasons: the honeymoon, early years of marriage, the season of having children, the season of grandparenting, and more. As a couple, you want to be aware of the challenges and joys of the season you are in, and as Paul said, make the most of each season.

LEADER: More information on time in the New Testament: We get *chronological* or *chronology* from the Greek word *chronos* (examples include Matthew 2:7; Acts 17:30; 1 Peter 1:17). *Kairos*, meaning more like a "season" of time, or a critical moment, is the focus here. We see its meaning in Romans 13:11–13 where Paul says, "you know the time," where he means "you are aware of the season we are in." For the marriage, this means: (1) awareness of the fact that our culture does not honor biblical marriage and understand our need to swim against the current, and (2) taking advantage of critical times or seasons where we focus on cultivating our marriage or reviewing the foundation. We call this a teachable moment with children, but we need those too. It's a reminder that when you go through a hard time, it is just a season, not your whole marriage. It's also a reminder to note those seasons when you are close, growing, and enjoying each other!

NOTE: *Chronos* is found about fifty-four times in the New Testament, but *kairos* is used eighty-six times. Understanding the significance of a certain time or season is an important New Testament idea.

REVIEW

Pray with and for one another daily (Matthew 18:19–20). Rate of divorce less than 1 percent.

Love your spouse as *he or she* desires to be loved with God's love (1 John 4:19–21; Ephesians 5:33).

Evangelize one another (1 Peter 3:1–2; Ephesians 5:25–27).

Ask how can I love you more (Philippians 2:2–4)?

S Is for Study

1. **Invest in your relationship with God through the daily study of God's Word.** The more intimate your relationship with Christ, the more your life and marriage will bear the fruits of the Spirit. His commands are not burdens to us when we are filled with His Spirit. Daily fellowship and prayer are the foundation of your marriage! (1 John 5:3; Mark 1:35; Galatians 5:16, 22; John 7:38)

How do we not conform to the world but instead be transformed? (Review of Romans 12:1–2)

Your marriage will not look exactly as you dreamt it would. Your spouse will not always meet your expectations. You will see their weakness more often than you would like.

However, if you allow, God can take those unrealized expectations and make something beautiful! He wants to bless you both with abundant life (John 10:10)—a life that is beyond your wildest dreams. But remember, He has a desire for us to be holy, and that often requires a degree of discomfort. If you allow Him, He will use your marriage as a method of sanctification to transform you, to bring you closer to what He desires you to be. This might be painful at times but will result in holiness in your life that you would likely never be able to attain otherwise.

Based on the paragraph above, how can Matthew 16:24–25; Luke 22:42; and Proverbs 3:5–6 apply to your marriage?

_____

_____

_____

_____

_____

2. You need to continue to have a habit of studying your spouse.

What is important to them? What makes them feel your love? What are their favorite foods and activities? Continue dating after marriage and remember that there will be many seasons of learning and growth.

GROUP DISCUSSION

Read Philippians 2:2–4. List the statements describing how to treat one another.

_____

_____

_____

_____

_____

How is it possible for you to live this passage out in your marriage?

_____

_____

_____

_____

_____

Deeper in the Word

Philippians 2:2–4

Background

Paul concludes Philippians 1 by exhorting the Philippian church to stay strong in the face of outside pressure and persecution. Chapter 2 turns the focus to inner attitudes believers should exhibit. He mentioned unity in 1:27; here he unpacks what that unity looks like. Paul lays a foundation for unity in verse 1; in verses 2–4, he describes a reason for unity (v. 2a) followed by a description of it (vv. 2b–4). These verses are all one lengthy sentence in the Greek text, with "one basic command: 'Make my joy complete.' "[26]

These verses show how to both develop healthy relationships and work through strained ones. They give a template for

---

26 Richard R. Melick, *Philippians, Colossians, Philemon*, The New American Commentary, vol. 32 (Nashville: Broadman & Holman, 1991), 92.

a healthy marriage and the tools to restore fellowship when tension arises, as it inevitably will.

Supporting passages: Acts 16:11–40; Philippians 1:21; 1 Peter 5:5*b*–7.

Investigation

Paul introduces this chapter pronouncing the blessing of Christian community. In verse 1, Paul's expression "if" does not express doubt but could be translated as *since* or *assuming that* four things are true for believers: (1) we are encouraged from our relationship with Christ; (2) we are comforted by his love; (3) we enjoy fellowship with the Spirit; and (4) we have mercies from God ("tenderness and compassion").

Verse 2: "Complete my joy." Though Paul is in prison when he writes this letter, it is filled with joy, with no less than sixteen mentions of the word. Paul planted this church and faced many challenges in doing so (Acts 16). His love for this church is clear throughout the epistle. "Complete" means to "fill full."

Three actions by the Philippians would produce the joy Paul describes:

1. **"Being of the same mind."** Paul uses this expression ten times in Philippians: "It incorporates the will and emotions into a comprehensive outlook which affects the attitude. With this word and the contexts in which it occurs, Paul spoke of the values and ambitions which surface through the mind. This is unity. It is not found in an identical lifestyle or personality. It occurs when Christian people have the same values and loves. Paul sought that in this church."[27]

---

27 Melick, *Philippians, Colossians, Philemon,* 164.

This doesn't mean to agree about everything, but it does mean there is unity of mind on things that matter. There is a difference between *unity*, which comes from a shared purpose and affection, and *uniformity*, which comes from outside pressure, or *conformity* in all things whether trivial or vital. The motive for unity is to have the same mind as Jesus (see Philippians 2:5) because believers are "in Christ" (v. 1).

Believers can be walk in unity and have different opinions on a lot of things, from sports teams to music styles (including in church), to a political opinion.

2. "Having the same love." We are to develop within and display without the love of Jesus Christ, which Paul will describe powerfully in 2:5–11 where he shows Jesus to be the ultimate model of humility and love.

3. "Being in full accord and of one mind." This means one with other believers in purpose.

Verse 3: Verses 3 and 4 each offer a contrast to show what unity looks like with a negative statement followed by a positive one.

"Do nothing from selfish ambition or conceit." This is what pride looks like. It is the opposite of humility. Selfish ambition plagues us all and must be recognized when it rears its ugly head.

The Greek term for *conceit* is a combination of "vain" or "empty" and the word *doxos* or "glory." Glorifying ourselves is an empty practice.

"But in humility count others more significant than yourselves." Humility is the same term used in Matthew 11:29

where we see Jesus describing himself as "gentle and lowly in heart." This has the idea of values and that a core value for a Christian in relationship with others is to count them more important than ourselves.

"More significant" is literally "excel" and is also used by Paul in Philippians 3:8 where he counts nothing of more value than "the surpassing worth of knowing Christ." Humility can only happen when a person's identity rests in Jesus Christ. We have nothing to prove, only Someone to please!

This is so important to Paul that he gives four examples of humility in the rest of chapter 2: the supreme example of Jesus (2:5–11); Paul himself (2:12–18); Timothy (2:19–24); and Epaphroditus (2:25–30).

In our polarized world, too often people (including Christians) define those who believe differently from us by their beliefs first rather than starting with the realization they are, like us, created in the image of God. If we start relationships with others on the basis that people were created by God and that Jesus died for them, it can impact how we treat others and develop greater humility in us.

Verse 4: "Let each of you look not only to his own interests." Again, a negative statement first. "Look" means to fix one's attention on something. This is the opposite of constantly jockeying for a position, seeking our way first.

Notice it doesn't say we aren't to look at all to our own interests. When one person always gets what he or she wants and the other always yields, there will be problems. The point here is to be other-person centered rather than focusing on oneself.

"But also to the interests of others." This is the idea of being considerate. In the church, this means we value every person as being an important part of the body of Christ regardless of their past or their position. As Paul is directing this to a church, this includes the idea that if one member of the church had a concern it would be the concern of all.[28]

Importance

People can steal our joy. Ironically, the people most likely to do so are the people closest to us. Married couples know both the joy they have in their bond but also recognize at times joy can be elusive when there is friction in the marriage. These verses give us the hope as believing couples you can "work together for the same purposes rather than seeking areas of disagreement and division."[29] For a married couple, this means single-mindedness on things that matter (v. 2) and a submissive mind (v. 3).

We basically learn two ways: by similitude and by contrast. That is, we learn by seeing things we want to imitate (similitude): "In humility count others more significant than yourself" (v. 3) and "look . . . to the interests of others" (v. 4) are examples to follow here. Contrast means doing the opposite: "Do nothing from selfish ambition or conceit" (v. 3) and "look not only to [your] own interests" (v. 4) show this contrast. This means a simple pattern of our discipleship is this: as we study the Bible

---

28 Melick, *Philippians, Colossians, Philemon*, 164.

29 Max Anders, *Galatians, Ephesians, Philippians & Colossians*, Holman New Testament Commentary (Nashville: Broadman & Holman, 1999), 224.

and as we face issues in our lives and our marriages, we can ask ourselves this: (1) What attitude/action should I be displaying that is consistent with God's Word (similitude); (2) What attitude/action should I stop because it is not consistent with God's Word (contrast). The more we know the Scriptures the more we can do this in everyday life.

Paul's use of the word *humility* shows the countercultural nature of the Christian faith. Before the New Testament, the term *humility* was not a virtue but was seen only negatively. It described a person who was of no value, like a slave.[30] But the New Testament turns that idea on its head. For the believer, the way to win at life is to surrender everything to Jesus; the way to find life is to die to oneself; the way to self-fulfillment is in serving others; and the way of relationships is humility. You do not see this magnified in a culture that glorifies making a name for yourself, gaining "likes" on social media, and getting revenge when wronged.

You will not learn how to thrive in marriage from the world system. Only living to God's glory, growing in the Word through the power of the Spirit, and living life for Jesus will pull you from the drift into the joy Paul describes in Philippians.

Implications

Unity in marriage is vital but also easily challenged. A Christian married couple represents two redeemed people brought together in covenant; but though redeemed, they are still prone to selfishness!

---

30 Philip Yancey, *The Jesus I Never Knew* (Grand Rapids: Zondervan, 2002), 36.

Think of something you hate, something that stirs your righteousness to do something. It could be the evil of child abuse, the sin of racism, or the plague of drug addiction. Whatever it is, none of us hate anything evil to the level that God hates pride: "God opposes the proud but gives grace to the humble" (1 Peter 5:5*b*). God is in opposition to pride, reflected in selfish ambition and conceit. But God gives grace to the humble. If you want to see the grace of God on your marriage, treat one another with humility and honor.

We are by nature selfish. Even as redeemed believers, we will battle wanting our way more than God's way or the wishes of others. This passage offers a powerful call to die to self and put others first. In marriage, this is essential. If your purpose as a couple is to follow the Lord and serve one another more than seeking your own desires, you will display what these verses describe.

How can we do this? Remember this: living the Christian life is not hard. It is *impossible*! Except for the grace of God, that is. We can only do this as we daily surrender afresh to God and embrace humility toward each other.

A growing marriage will continue to identify issues that cause friction with this purpose. One of the most important things husbands and wives can do is to be curious when friction comes. Asking why our spouse's action made us feel the way it did is important, as is asking why getting our way over putting our spouse first is so important to us. Because we tend to become selfish when we feel insecure, it could be our lack of security in our identity in Christ (see 1 Peter 2:9). Exploring together why attitudes and actions arise that hinder a couple's unity is an important part of growing together.

Most of the time when we get angry, it's because we don't get our way. We won't drift into the attitude of putting our spouse first and looking out for his/her interests. We constantly choose to imitate Jesus. Reading Philippians 2:1–11 as a couple each day for one week can help build this passage into your marriage.

Seeking to be unified as a couple marks one of the priorities of a marriage as it does for a local church.

We all ultimately want what Paul wants: for our joy to be full. That's not a selfish request because joy is something God wants for us. We see joy as a theme throughout Scripture. (It is mentioned over four hundred times!) Psalms 4:7; 30:5; John 16:22; and 1 Peter 1:8–9 are just a few of the many verses on joy.

In the New Testament, the terms *joy*, *gratitude/thanksgiving*, and *grace* are all from the same Greek root. When we live aware of God's amazing grace in our lives (*charis*), we will be grateful (*eucharisto*), which brings us joy (*chara*).[31]

And that way of life will value humility, putting our spouse first, and serving in love.

E Is for Example

3. Finally, your marriage should be an example to a lost world and point them to Christ. He created marriage to bless you, give you intimacy, to raise godly children, and to further His kingdom and purpose. Decide whether your marriage will draw others to Christ (including your children), or if it will draw others away from

---

31 Alvin Reid, *Restoring Gratitude: Finding Beauty in a Broken World* (Be Inspired Books, 2020), kindle location 1037.

Him. Decide what you want the foundation of your marriage to be. You get to decide—rock or sand?

Read James 1:22. Discuss how this verse shows that how you "live out" your marriage determines your witness to a lost world.

> **LEADER:** Encourage the group to think about the spiritual markers they've seen in the past, those times when God answered prayer, took you through a difficult season, and others. These spiritual markers are examples of God's faithfulness. Remember and celebrate what God has done in your marriage. As you focus on your God-given success, it leads you to a closer relation with one another. God uses these markers to encourage you and encourage other believers well.

Review and Application

Review what the foundation of your marriage will be, including these key ideas:

P—Pray together; this is critical to your marriage.

1. Have you begun praying daily together? If so, what have you learned so far? If you are still working toward this, what might the main issues be that hinder you from praying together?

_____

_____

_____

_____

_____

L—Love one another unconditionally, as God loves us.

2. Do you think daily first of loving your spouse or of your own needs? How might you show love to one another this week?

_____

_____

_____

_____

_____

E—Evangelize one another, reminding each other of the good news.

3. What are ways the gospel can help you to encourage one another this week? Ideas: Jesus forgave us far more than we will ever have to forgive; we received amazing grace from God; we have been redeemed for a purpose; because we know God, we have the power to serve Him personally and in our marriage through the Spirit; etc.

_____

_____

_____

_____

_____

A—Ask each other how you can help your spouse feel more loved.

4. What are some simple ways you can ask one another about this?

_____

_____

_____

_____

_____

S—Study God's Word and one another.

5. Can you share something you learned from God's Word this week with your spouse that's helped you to know and serve the Lord more effectively?

_____

_____

_____

_____

E—Example: Be an example to the world through your marriage.

6. How can you pray and ask God to help you to be a godly example in your marriage?

_____

_____

_____

_____

_____

BIBLICAL FOUNDATION: THE HUSBAND, PART 1

Ephesians 5:25–30

> **LEADER:** The beginning of the group is a good time to encourage couples to pray together daily. You might poll the group during the week to find a couple who has already begun to see the impact of praying together daily; consider asking them to share briefly with the group. If you have men who travel frequently, here is a word for them:
>
> If you travel, you can be very vulnerable when you travel and not realize it. You can really get in the world when you travel, so having prayer time with your wife when you travel is a big deal. When you've got some private or alone time, pick up the phone and call your wife and pray with her over the phone.

Compare and contrast how the world views the role of the husband in family and society versus the biblical view.

> **LEADER:** On a marker board or flipchart make two columns, one marked WORLD and the other marked BIBLE. Write down the responses to the discussion above. You may find that learners can list far more on the world side than the Bible.

Where do we find the TRUTH of the role of the man in marriage? (2 Timothy 3:16–17; Romans 12:2; and Hebrews 4:12)

The primary responsibility of the husband in the Christian home is to lead as God's Word instructs us. Husbands, you are to love your wife, not as the world loves, but as Christ loves the church and gave Himself for her. This is a sacrificial, self-denying kind of love. Your role as head or leader of your home does not give you the right to dominate and control but to lead like Jesus. To do that, we must be surrendered to Jesus ourselves.

1. **The husband must FIRST __submit__ to Christ and experience God's unconditional love in His own life** (Luke 10:27).

> **LEADER:** You might point out to the men that in our culture we are encouraged to put on armor and to avoid vulnerability: Remember when you were a little boy on the playground, if you showed any emotion, what happened to you? You got beat up, or at best you got taunted.
>
> But if we are to be one with our wives as God intended, we will need to open up to our wives. We will never experience a deep relationship with God if we won't be honest with God about our struggles, our pain, and our need for Him. Then we can experience the depth of His love.

2. **The husband must be __intentional__.** He is to know and understand his role. The primary ambition in his life is to love God, and to love his wife unconditionally. He understands the Holy Spirit is the source of his love, strength, wisdom, and guidance. If he relies on the culture or his male instincts to direct him, he will fail miserably.

He understands the authority and responsibility given to him by God to serve, lead, and sacrifice for his wife and family.

He (1) rejects passivity, (2) leads courageously, and (3) accepts responsibility. He does NOT conform to this culture and worldview as we saw in Romans 12:2.

Time + Unintentionality = Failure

3. The husband is to love his wife as Christ loved the church and gave himself for her (Ephesians 5:25).

He loves by:

LEADER: Point out that Ephesians 5 is crucial in our study. Ephesians is not primarily a corrective book but a preventative one. The first three chapters are instructional, telling us our identity in Christ and how we are part of God's family, the Church. The final three chapters give detailed, practical wisdom on how to live out who we are.

Once each blank is filled in, feel free to restate the questions that follow to facilitate discussion. Take your time on these as each statement may impact different people.

Note also that *love* here is *agape*, the kind of love Jesus showed on the cross.

ILLUSTRATION: Imagine a bull's-eye: you may not always hit it, but at least it gives you something to aim for. We won't always hit the ideal for marriage, but Ephesians, in particular, and all God's Word will give us the target to aim for.

A. Unconditional _love_ (Ephesians 5:25–27). Do you love unconditionally?

> **LEADER:** You can note here that the world tends to see love as acceptance without consequences, or often just as a feeling or emotion. But Ephesians 5:25 is extremely clear in its understanding of how husbands are to love their wives: as Christ loved the church. How did He love the church? He gave Himself for her. Husbands sacrifice like Jesus. Husbands forgive like Jesus. Husbands serve like Jesus.
>
> Practically, this may look like this: We pray, "God, help me not to love my wife based on whether she cooks a great meal or cleans the house like I want, or is always available for sexual intimacy. Help me to love her unconditionally."

What are ways you've been taught or shown how to love your wife in the past? How do those compare to how Jesus loves His bride?

B. Learning what makes her _happy_ (Deuteronomy 24:5). What are things you know that make her happy? Is this something you need to learn more from her?

> **LEADER:** This may be a topic some couples have never discussed. Point out that all couples have a learning curve here, and husbands will learn this more clearly as they make this a priority. Encourage husbands to take some time to ask their wives this question during the week (and listen to what she says!).

C. Leaving and _cleaving_ (Genesis 2:24). Do you know how to be "one" with your wife?

D. Protecting _her_ (Mark 3:27; 1 John 4:18). Do you know what makes her feel safe?

> **LEADER:** Often husbands have one idea of what safety looks like, and the wife has a different idea. You might give each person a card and ask each spouse to answer these questions respectively: WIFE, what makes you feel safe? HUSBAND, what makes your wife feel safe? Go over the answers, encouraging each spouse not to see the different answers as a problem but an opportunity to understand one another better.

E. _Loving_ and cherishing (Ephesians 5:28–29). Do you know what your wife needs?

Read John 14:15; 14:21; 1 John 5:3. It is of utmost importance to love God first and most—to love Him and obey Him. If you don't love your wife, it is usually because you have stopped loving God.

How can these verses help motivate the Christian husband?

_____

_____

_____

_____

_____

> **ILLUSTRATION:** Too many marriages function almost like a game of tennis: the husband is on one side of the net and hits the tennis ball. She's on the other side hitting tennis ball back, volleying back and forth:
>
> **Serve:** "If you love me this way, then I'll do this for you."
> **Return:** "If you do that for me, I'll do this for you."
>
> Is that love? No, it's manipulation and selfishness. And joy will never come from this.

John's Story

In our thirty years of marriage, we've seen this. At one point my pride had us far apart emotionally, but over the course of several years we saw that gap closing, so that after five years we were much closer. That's the beauty of marriage because the more you become one, the more you become known and love together, the more you'll see so many beautiful things come out of your marriage and so many discoveries of different seasons of life. The energy that fulfills all that, everything that makes that run, is your spiritual connection. We learned this from the simple, daily practice of praying together. When we were in the depths of our marriage, when our marriage was really bad for the first ten plus years, Julie really didn't want to pray with me sometimes even after we started praying together. There was a breakdown of trust. Sometimes I would just hold her on the shoulder and pray over her. But over time, as the days and weeks passed, she really warmed up to it so much. And now we're at a point where we won't go a day without praying together. I'd be afraid to, to be honest.

If he loves God, he will love his ___wife___ as Christ loves the church. How did Christ love the church? He gave Himself for her (sacrificial love, Ephesians 5:25). If he does not love God, he will ___not___ love his wife unconditionally. *His priorities and motivation will be from God, not man or what he feels.*

4. He is the ___head___ of his wife as "Christ is head of the church." This is an *unconditional* statement whether he realizes it or not. He is the head of his family (1 Corinthians 11:3; Ephesians 5:23). Headship is translated in Greek as *kephale* and often means the physical head of the body, the cornerstone of a building, or an authority figure. *Kephale* can also mean the "source" as in the source of a spring.[32] Headship means that everything that flows into the marriage/family will come through the husband. This means that he is responsible for his marriage for his family. If there is any dysfunction in his marriage and family, it is almost always traced back to the man and his role as husband and father. God will hold the husband accountable for his marriage and his family. Just as Jesus was called to love, give, and sacrifice for the church as head, so the husband is called to love, give, and sacrifice for his marriage as Christ did as the head in His marriage.

LEADER: A deeper dive into *kephale*:

The husband as head of the home is unpopular today and often misunderstood in the church. Here is greater clarity gleaned from pastor Sam Storms.[33]

---

32 John R. Markley, "Head of the Church," ed. John D. Barry et al., *The Lexham Bible Dictionary* (Bellingham, WA: Lexham, 2016).

33 Sam Storms, "10 Things You Should Know About Male Headship," Sam Storms (blog), https://www.samstorms.org/all-articles/post/article-10-things-you-should-know-about-male-headship.

1. The husband is *not* the ruler of his wife: The Bible says the husband is to love his wife, not rule her (Ephesians 5:25).

2. The husband is not superior: Headship is not for self-exaltation but is other-oriented. Any attitude or action that makes the husband superior and the wife inferior is inconsistent with Scripture. But abusing headship is no grounds for abandoning the biblical concept.

3. The husband as head has greater responsibilities, not greater rights: It is a sacred trust from God.

4. The husband has the authority to serve: This follows the example of Jesus (Mark 10:45).

5. The husband as head is called to *lead*: We lead best as we seek to be like Jesus most. This does not mean the husband makes all decisions unilaterally, as wives also have wisdom, and calling on the wife to make a decision does not undermine his role.

6. The husband as head is the biblical norm: Husbands must lead consistently with Scripture and not contrary to it.

7. The husband is to lead with gentleness and sensitivity: Colossians 3:19 warns husbands not to be "harsh" toward them (ESV; CSV says "do not abuse them").

Take-Home Discussion for the Husband

Husband, it is your role in headship to build a safe place where you and your wife can have deep, intimate conversation without fear of punishment and where you are both secure enough to speak without taking things personally. These questions reflect the lesson and offer a place to discuss these during the week.

> **LEADER:** Stress how vital it is to discuss these with the perspective of learning more about one another and how to love each other better and to resist the temptation to see these as grounds for criticism.

Ask your wife:

1. What do I do that makes you feel love?

_____

_____

_____

_____

_____

2. What do I do that makes you happy?

_____

_____

_____

_____

3. What do I do that makes you feel "oneness" with me?

_____

_____

_____

_____

4. What do I do that makes you feel safe?

_____

_____

_____

_____

_____

5. What is one fruit of the Spirit that you would like to pray for me?

_____

_____

_____

_____

_____

These questions are a good starting point to have a positive discussion on how to be the husband God called you to be. Try not to be discouraged or overwhelmed by this discussion. Knowledge is power. How can you know if she never shares with you? Remember, you are on the same team. She is for you! When you love one another, you are actually loving yourself. You are "one flesh."

BIBLICAL FOUNDATION:
THE HUSBAND, PART 2

Ephesians 5:25–30

Deeper in the Word

Ephesians 5:25–28

Background

Paul begins this chapter with the admonishment to imitate God, followed by a number of practical ways to do that as believers. We are to do so as obedient children. The analogy makes sense as he will spend time in chapters 5 and 6 on the family and relationships between husband, wife, and children. We have the capacity to imitate God because He fills us with the Holy Spirit (v. 18). Paul makes it clear that being filled by the Spirit will impact how we relate to others and not just how we act each Sunday in church services. How we treat one another in the home is a clear indication of how seriously we take imitating God and being led by the Spirit.

Supporting passages: Colossians 3:18–20; 1 Peter 3:1–7.

Investigation

Verse 25: "Husbands, love your wives, as Christ loved the church and gave himself up for her." For Paul there is no ambiguity: a husband is a male and a wife a female, and marriage consists of a man and a woman joined together in marriage.

Paul "instructs husbands to love their wives so completely and so righteously that the wife need never fear or suffer from her life of submission."[34]

He gives three critical ideas: First, husbands are to *love their wives*. This is a command; it is not optional. Second, *how* they are to love their wives is clear, as Christ loved the church. Third, to make it even more clear, this is how Christ loved the church: *"He gave himself up for her."* There is no higher level of love a man could attain for his wife than to love her as Christ loved the church.

"Love" is *agape*, which is love that pursues the highest good for the other person, demonstrated most perfectly in Christ's death for us (John 3:16; Romans 5:8).

The husband "is to dedicate his life to the physical, emotional, and spiritual welfare of his wife. Following the example of Christ, he is to give his wife not only all that he has but also all that he is. When a husband loves his wife so completely, the wife need never fear submission."[35] No greater description of this kind of love can be found than in the verses in 1 Corinthians 13: **"Love is patient and kind; love does not envy or boast; it**

---

34 Max Anders, *Galatians, Ephesians, Philippians & Colossians*, Holman New Testament Commentary (Nashville: Broadman & Holman, 1999), 174.

35 Anders, *Galatians, Ephesians, Philippians & Colossians*, 174.

is not arrogant or rude. It does not insist on its own way; it is not irritable or resentful; it does not rejoice at wrongdoing, but rejoices with the truth. Love bears all things, believes all things, hopes all things, endures all things" (1 Corinthians 13:4–7).

Verse 26: "That he might sanctify her, having cleansed her by the washing of water with the word." Jesus prayed for His disciples to be sanctified in truth from God's Word (John 17:17). Husbands, as spiritual leaders in the home, have this same desire for their wives.

"Sanctify her." This means "to set apart."

> In the marriage ceremony, the husband is set apart to belong to the wife, and the wife is set apart to belong to the husband. Any interference with this God-given arrangement is sin. Today, Christ is cleansing His church through the ministry of His Word (John 15:3; 17:17). The love of the husband for his wife ought to be cleansing her (and him) so that both are becoming more like Christ.[36]

"Cleansed" is the word from which we get "catharsis." This is metaphorical, as in the example of Christ's loving the church to the point of dying for her.

"Washing of water with the word." This word is *rhema*, which "refers to the 'preached Word' that unbelievers hear."[37] Most interpreters believe this refers to baptism with water. Baptism

---

36 Warren W. Wiersbe, *Be Rich: Gaining the Things that Money Can't Buy* (Colorado Springs: David C. Cook, 1979), 51.

37 Harold W. Hoehner, "Ephesians" in *The Bible Knowledge Commentary: An Exposition of the Scriptures*, vol. 2, eds. John F. Walvoord, Roy B. Zuck (Wheaton, IL: Victor Books, 1985), 641.

in the New Testament does not literally cleanse a person but symbolizes the inner work of salvation for one who has repented and believed.

Verse 27: "So that he might present the church." The same idea is found in 2 Corinthians 11:2 concerning presenting the bride to the bridegroom. Paul compares the relationship with Jesus as the bridegroom to the church, His bride.

"Holy and without blemish." This is both positive (holy, set apart to God) and negative (without blemish/stain). This same expression is used in Ephesians 1:4 as Paul describes our election as believers.

Verse 28: "In the same way husbands should love their wives as their own bodies. He who loves his wife loves himself." Paul gives a second comparison for husbands. First, they are to love their wives as Christ loved the church. Now, they are to love their wives as they love their own bodies. In marriage, a husband and a wife become one flesh, so the husband who does not love his wife is not loving himself either. "Just as love is the circulatory system of the body of Christ (Eph. 4:16), so love is the nourishment of the home."[38]

Importance

There is no higher love than the love Jesus showed us on the cross. His love for the church, giving Himself for her (v. 25) reveals the standard husbands have for love toward their wives. Nothing a husband loves compares to his love for his wife.

---

38 Warren W. Wiersbe, *The Bible Exposition Commentary*, vol. 2 (Wheaton, IL: Victor Books, 1996), 51.

The wife is to *submit* to her husband's leadership. Men need respect.

The husband is to love his wife *sacrificially*: women need to be loved.

How then does the husband lead the home? " 'As unto Christ' is the motive. Wives are to submit to their husbands as unto Christ; husbands are to love their wives as Christ loves the church; and children are to obey as unto the Lord. Family members who are right with the Lord will be right with each other."[39]

Implications

This passage explicitly speaks of the work of the Spirit in marriage and implies the importance of God's Word. The parallel passage in Colossians highlights the Word.

1. *Spirit-filled marriage:* It is vital to see that these practical instructions for the home follow after Paul's call to be continually filled with the Spirit (Ephesians 5:18). He says in that verse not to be "drunk with wine" but to be filled instead with the Holy Spirit. There is no way we would affirm a husband who is a drunkard, and most of us know tragic stories of abuse and violence because of drunken husbands and fathers. But Paul is saying something more that we often miss. It is wrong to be drunk, but how much worse is it for a believer not to be walking in the fullness of the Spirit of God who lives within us? It is only through the Spirit's work that wives can submit to their husbands (v. 22) and husbands love their wives as Christ loved the church.

---

39 Wiersbe, *Bible Exposition Commentary*, 52.

2. *Word-filled marriage:* In a parallel passage in Colossians 3:16 Paul says to "Let the word of Christ dwell in you richly." As he did in Ephesians, Paul then gives instructions on marriage. For marriages to thrive, both husband and wife are to be Spirit-filled and Word-guided.

Husbands are to love their wives, but how? Paul gives us the example: "as Christ loved the church and gave himself for her" (Ephesians 5:25).

LEADER: Remind couples that one of the specific goals for this curriculum is to help them to have a "Starbucks moment" every week. This is the moment to say, "OK, how am I doing as a husband? How are you doing? What have I done this week that's hurt you? How am I doing as a father? What do we need to pray for?" That's when you have your moment to say, "Hey, when you did this, it really hurt my feelings." Or "Hey, why don't we ever do this anymore?"

Husbands, what were some helpful things you learned from your take-home discussion?

_____

_____

_____

_____

_____

> **LEADER:** Consider checking in with couples during the week to see if you can identify those couples who would share insights that helped them through the exercise or simply ask for volunteers to share. Remind couples that doing this is a positive step to foster growth. Take some time to review this as by now you want the group to be open and honest in their discussions.

What does *headship* mean for the husband according to the New Testament?

_____

_____

_____

_____

_____

How does that compare with culture today?

_____

_____

_____

_____

_____

> **LEADER:** List the differences on the board. Remind couples that God's design for marriage goes all the way back to creation, and God's design has not changed. However, we live in a very

different place culturally, so Christian couples must recognize that pursuing God's design goes against the grain of society. This requires devotion to and dependence on God.

Examples of headship in marriage: Genesis 3:6; Philippians 2:7–8; Romans 5:19.

We can see the contrast in Romans 5:19 between two husbands and their legacies. Adam (the first "one man" listed) brought the legacy of sin, but Jesus (the second) brings a legacy of righteousness. A husband or father who does not exercise headship in a kind, gentle, selfless manner slanders God and jeopardizes not only his own eternity but also those who are closest to him.

LEADER: Take time to dig into Romans 5:19 to contrast Adam, the first husband, with Jesus, the husband to the church. Remind the group that God told Adam not to eat of the tree of the knowledge of good and evil BEFORE He created Eve (Genesis 2:15–18). And although Eve took the fruit and gave it to Adam, when God looked for them in the garden, who did He call out to? Adam, the head (Genesis 3:9).

C. S. Lewis said, "This headship, then, is most fully embodied not in the husband we should all wish to be but in him whose marriage is most like a crucifixion; whose wife receives most and gives least, is most unworthy of him, is—in her own mere nature—least lovable. For the Church has no beauty but what the Bride-groom gives her; he does not find, but makes her, lovely."[40]

---

40 C. S. Lewis, *The Four Loves: The Much Beloved Exploration of the Nature of Love* (Orlando: Harcourt, 1960), 105.

1. **The husband is _responsible_ for his marriage and family.** He will be held accountable for the salvation and direction of his marriage/family. As the man goes, so goes his family. When a man follows God and submits to God's leadership, his family follows after him (Ephesians 6:4; Colossians 3:2).

2. **He is to be the _teacher_ of his children** (Ephesians 6:4; Colossians 3:21).

> **LEADER:** Note that this of course does not omit the role of the mother in teaching, as Deuteronomy 6:4–9 places teaching at the feet of both parents. But too often husbands fail to take seriously their role here.

> Statistics from fatherless homes: 5 times more likely to commit suicide, 9 times more likely to drop out of high school, 20 times more likely to end up in jail. [41]

Discuss the spiritual impact of men fulfilling or not fulfilling God's role in Christian marriage and in society.

> **LEADER:** List the responses on the board and discuss individually, then how collectively all the examples given bring harm. In our culture, husbands are often an afterthought in the home and almost treated as invisible or unnecessary.
>
> Much of the chaos of society comes from the failure of men to take the role God gave us. Women in the feminist movement hate men and are against men. They've only seen men who are

---

41 "Research and Statistics," Rochester Area Fatherhood Network, http://www.rochesterareafatherhoodnetwork.org/statistics.

like Adam. They've never had anybody love them like Christ loves.

It's not their fault; it's our fault as men. It starts in your bedroom, in your house with your wife. It's what God calls us to do. You'll never feel more alive than when you love your wife like Jesus loves the church.

There's nothing greater than to see your wife walking with God, growing closer to God, in a vital, active relationship with Christ. There's nothing more fulfilling than to see your love sacrificially for her, loving her as Christ loves the church.

3. The way he treats his wife affects his relationship with God (1 Peter 3:7; Malachi 2:13–15).

LEADER: Note specifically how 1 Peter 3:7 reveals a direct relationship between a husband and his wife and his personal prayer life. Remind couples that if they are in Christ, their relationship with God eternally is secure. However, our daily intimacy with God is affected by both our vertical relationship with God and our horizontal relationship with others. Our relationship with our spouse is the most crucial horizontal relationship.

4. Even Christlike husbands will stumble (Psalm 37:23–24; Proverbs 24:16; Isaiah 41:10). We will stumble and that's okay. We want to keep learning and growing. Jesus is the only one who never sinned!

LEADER: This is good place to encourage husbands who are aware of their failures yet want to make a fresh start. Proverbs

24:16 is especially powerful: the righteous will fall but rise again. Get up! God uses broken people; we are all He has!

5. It is a ___daily___ walk. Your level of spiritual maturity and ministry will never exceed your role as husband (Matthew 6:33; John 15:7; Philippians 3:13–14). What will your legacy be as a husband?

Just as we discussed, God made male and female very different, so expect a time of learning and adjustment. But remember, YOU are responsible for your marriage and family.

A Reminder of God's Kind of Love

Love is ___patient___ and ___kind___; love does not ___envy___ or boast; it is not ___arrogant___ or rude. It does not ___insist___ on its own way; it is not irritable or ___resentful___; it does not rejoice at ___wrongdoing___, but rejoices with the ___truth___. Love ___bears___ all things, ___believes___ all things, hopes all things, ___endures___ all things. (1 Corinthians 13:4–7)

"*Love* is to put yourself in the place of another, to feel their feelings, walk in their shoes, weep with their tears, rejoice in their joys, take upon yourself their burdens, and give to them your life. . . . When you feel it and when you don't, it doesn't matter—it doesn't change anything. . . . We can only receive it and be changed by it. We can only let it change us."[42]

---

42 Jonathan Cahn, *The Book of Mysteries* (Lake Mary, FL: Frontline, 2018), day 12.

THE ROLE OF THE CHRISTIAN WIFE

Ephesians 5:22–24

Compare and contrast how the world views the role of the wife in family and society versus the biblical view. Where do we find the TRUTH of the role of the woman in marriage (Ephesians 5:33; Genesis 2:18)?

The primary responsibility of the wife in the Christian home is to respect and submit to her husband. She was created to be her husband's helpmate. She intercedes for her husband through prayer, submission, and respect through the power of the Holy Spirit in her life. God designed her role to be one of strength, which is of utmost importance in her life and the life of her husband.

LEADER

Deeper in the Word

Ephesians 5:22–24, 33

Background

These verses in Ephesians 5 focus specifically on wisdom for wives.

Investigation

Verse 22: "Wives, submit to your own husbands." Note that this is in the context of a Christian wife and her believing husband. The term *submit* is a military term, which literally means "to be under in rank."[43] This speaks not to value, talent, or intellect, but to respect for levels of rank. In verses 20 and 21, we read that husbands and wives are to submit first to Christ and then to each other, which means both husband and wife understand their value and the need to work together as a team. In this context then, Paul gives an order to the home, with the wife submitting to the husband, then children to their parents (Ephesians 6:1).

A wife submitting to her husband "does not mean that she submits to her husband in the same way and to the same degree as she does the Lord, since the husband might ask her to disobey God. Rather she serves the Lord by having a submissive heart toward her husband and by obeying him as long as it does not require her to disobey the Lord."[44]

The threat or fear of submitting to another person is the possibility of manipulation, mistreatment, or abuse. There are tragically many marriages in which this takes place. But the context here is a Christian wife and Christian husband, both of whom are earnest in their desire to live for Christ. Christ is head of the church (v. 23), and as we know Christ's attitude toward the church is love, so much that He gave Himself for her (v. 25).

43 David Guzik, "Ephesians 5—Life in the Spirit," Enduring Word Commentary, https://enduringword.com/bible-commentary/ephesians-5/.

44 Max Anders, *Galatians, Ephesians, Philippians & Colossians*, Holman New Testament Commentary (Nashville: Broadman & Holman, 1999), 173.

Therefore, a wife will submit to "her husband because he is the head of their relationship. The husband is the head of a marriage just as Christ is the head of the church."[45]

"*Submit* in modern English carries a connotation of giving in to arbitrary force. Nothing could be further from Paul's intention. He used a Greek word that related to the establishment of the social order."[46] The head of all Christian homes is Jesus Christ; the husband is the leader and protector of his family.

"Paul certainly does not imply that all (or any) husbands measure up to Christ in this regard, neither does he excuse wives from such submission because of the imperfection of their husbands."[47]

"As to the Lord." Husbands are to love their wives "as Christ loved the church" (v. 25). Similarly, wives are to submit to their husbands as they would to the Lord. This speaks to motive: a wife recognizes the husband's rank as leader out of respect to Jesus, who is Lord over them both.

"Each partner in a marriage has a privilege. The husband's privilege is to put his wife first, as Christ put us first when He died for us. The wife's privilege is to set the tone of submission by being responsive and caring. Neither is 'over' the other; each ministers to the other in his or her special way."[48]

---

45 Andrew Knowles, *The Bible Guide* (Minneapolis: Augsburg, 2001), 620.

46 John B. Polhill, *Paul and His Letters* (Nashville: Broadman & Holman, 1999), 371.

47 Richard J. Erickson, "Ephesians," in *Evangelical Commentary on the Bible*, vol. 3, ed. Walter A. Elwell (Grand Rapids: Baker Books, 1995), 1030–31.

48 Lawrence O. Richards, *The Bible Reader's Companion*, electronic ed. (Wheaton, IL: Victor Books, 1991), 802.

Verse 23: "For the husband is the head of the wife even as Christ is the head of the church, his body, and is himself its Savior." Christ is head of the church, and the husband is the head of the wife. These two statements parallel; however, Christ alone is the Savior. The expression "is himself its Savior" refers only to Jesus, who is the Savior of the church.

Verse 24: "Now as the church submits to Christ, so also wives should submit in everything to their husbands." Paul restates the comparison between marriage and the church. Paul is giving two specific examples that compare husband and wife to Christ and the church. The husband is head of the wife like Christ is the head of the church (v. 23), and the wife submits to the husband as the church submits to Christ.

Verse 33*b*: "Let the wife see that she respects her husband." Studies show that respect is either the number one need or at the top of key needs of a husband.[49] Author Emerson Eggerisch found in his study that "men hear criticism as contempt while women feel silence as hostility."[50] Surely one of the key aspects of a growing Christian marriage is seen when both husband and wife learn how to express love, honor, and respect for one another.

---

49 Emerson Eggerichs, *Love and Respect: The Love She Most Desires; The Respect He Desperately Needs* (Nashville: Thomas Nelson, 2004). Also "4 Things Every Man Needs from His Wife," Lifeway, last modified May 8, 2013, https://www.lifeway .com/en/articles/homelife-men-women-4-things-every-man-needs-from-his -wife.

50 "Why Do Husbands Need Respect and Wives Desire Love?" Focus on the Family Singapore, last modified February 8, 2018, https://www.family.org.sg/fotfs/Blog /Marriage/Why_Do_Husbands_Need_Respect_and_Wives_Desire_Love .aspx.

Importance

Marriage, like other gifts from God, is a gift from God's grace. Marriage gives followers of Christ a pathway to demonstrate the essence of the Christian life, which is a life of service to God and others. It also lets us follow the example of Jesus, who said, "For even the Son of Man came not to be served but to serve, and to give his life as a ransom for many" (Mark 10:45).

A wife can show this servant's heart by submitting to the leadership of her husband. A husband can in turn show a servant's heart by loving his wife sacrificially. There are few (if any) things more valuable than for a wife to show how much she respects and appreciates her husband, just as (with Session Four) a husband showing how much he sacrificially loves his wife. The idea of submission to authority is essential in society: we submit to the authority of the police, our employer, a team's coach, a student's teacher, and so on.

These verses demonstrate the value of husbands and wives praying together daily, displaying a spirit of gratitude and appreciation for one another, and each being grounded and growing in the Word of God. Marital failure for believing couples often comes "from failure of the husband and or wife to submit to Christ, spend time in His Word, and seek to do His will each day."[51]

Implications

Paul gives three reasons for the wife to submit to the leadership of the husband: (1) the motive for doing so is to honor Jesus ("as

---

51 Warren W. Wiersbe, *The Bible Exposition Commentary*, vol. 2 (Wheaton, IL: Victor Books, 1996), 50.

to the Lord" verse 22); (2) God calls the husband the head of the wife as Christ is head of the church (v. 23); (3) as the church is subject to Christ, the wife is to her husband (v. 24).

We see the idea of submission in many realms in Scripture:[52]

- Jesus submitted to His parents (Luke 2:51).
- Demons submitted to the disciples (Luke 10:17).
- Citizens should submit to government authority (Romans 13:1, 5).
- Christians should submit to church leaders (Hebrews 13:17).
- Wives should submit to husbands (Ephesians 5:22–24; Colossians 3:18).
- The church should submit to Jesus (Ephesians 5:24).
- Servants should submit to masters (1 Peter 2:18).
- Christians should submit to God (James 4:7).

This passage illustrates why believers should not be "unequally yoked" (2 Corinthians 6:14) with unbelievers, particularly in the context of marriage. It would be difficult to expect an unbelieving spouse to follow these verses that are aimed at God's children.

Communication between spouses is essential here. Couples grow when they continue to learn more about each other, not so they can point out each other's flaws, but so that they can learn more helpful ways to show love and respect.

---

52 Guzik, "Ephesians 5—Life in the Spirit."

LEADER: Ask the group to talk about the pressures wives face today. Some examples include: unbiblical ideas about women, men, and their impact on wives; how marriage has become so diluted that we rarely hear of "wives" or "spouses" in advertisements or news, but we hear of "partners" instead; and some expectations of wives to be a kind of Wonder Woman who does everything well without ever complaining.

You can add that, in addition to these ideas, we all come into marriage with certain expectations that may or may not be biblical, and we may also forget that Satan wants to destroy our marriages.

1. You were created in the image of God to be an _*ezer kenegdo*_ to your husband (Genesis 1:27; Genesis 2:18).

ezer kenegdo—translated in Hebrew as *lifesaver*.

LEADER: A deeper dive into *ezer kenegdo*: *Ezer* was used by Moses to describe how God rescued him from Pharaoh (Exodus 18:4); *kenegdo* is "suitable" in the sense of completing something, like the North Pole is not complete without the South Pole.[53] It was "not good" when God first made Adam because he did not have a suitable helper who could be a lifesaver to him. And many husbands would testify that their wives have helped them like this.

As wives, we are to be a helper, or *ezer kenegdo*, for our husbands. *Ezer kenegdo* is translated in Hebrew as "lifesaver." The same Hebrew

---

53 K. A. Mathews, *Genesis 1–11:26*, vol. 1A, The New American Commentary (Nashville: Broadman & Holman, 1996), 214.

word in scripture used here for the woman is used elsewhere in the Bible only to refer to God the Father, God the Son, and God the Holy Spirit! It is a phrase of honor and significance, not an assignment to a lesser person or a second-class individual. God chose to use the same word for woman that He uses when describing God himself coming through for mankind ... when it is desperately needed and is a matter of life or death! What an exciting call on the life of a woman!

What are some ways we can "save" the lives of our husbands?

_____

_____

_____

_____

_____

_____

When you begin your marriage, you can hardly wait to set off on a new adventure—husband and wife ready to face life's ups and downs together. Similar to two people in a hot air balloon, you are excited to take off and begin your journey. You see your spouse through rose-colored glasses and are convinced you have married the Ferrari of all men. Surely all of your dreams will come true and many more!

ezer kenegdo ("life saver")
- Respect him.
- Speak words of life and encouragement.
- Pray for him.
- "Speak" his love language (physical affection).
- Thank him for all he does.

However, it does not take long to realize that our spouses are far from perfect (and we are too)! If you envision your marriage as a hot air balloon soaring high in the sky, you might be concerned when you begin to realize this hot air balloon has holes of imperfection. We begin to notice the flaws in our husband: angry outbursts, the messy floor, or a lack of attention to our needs. Slowly we see how what we thought was a Ferrari appears to be more of a Pinto!

He never helps at home.

He leaves clothes on the floor.

He has flaws (e.g., angry outbursts)

As wives, our first instinct is to point out the "holes of imperfection" in our balloon to our husbands. Minor irritations become large frustrations, and as we repeatedly share our thoughts on our husband's shortcomings, the holes in the balloon become larger. Over time, the balloon does not fly so well, and we are not sure why—all we did was point out the areas that "needed to be fixed"! Why does the entire balloon seem like it is about to crash?!

Have FAITH and BELIEVE
that God is working
miracles in your husband
and in your marriage.

When you build up your husband—**feed the "fire" of the Spirit**—
the hot air balloon takes off and you BOTH soar together.

Without the help of God's Word, we as wives think it is our job to point out the flaws and shortcomings in our husbands. And when he doesn't change, we think we need to speak louder, more frequently, and perhaps add in some eye-rolling or a slammed door.

We are then utterly frustrated when these antics do not make our lives better. Instead, we feel more distant from our husbands.

It is time to call for help! God's ways are so much better and higher than our ways! God wants us to pray over our husbands, believe the best about them, speak life over them, and have faith even when we can't see the outcome.

Here is our opportunity to be a lifesaver for our husbands, to see their potential, and to pray over their failures and weaknesses (the holes in the balloon). God wants us to act in faith, believe our husbands are in the process of becoming mighty men of God, and watch Him work miracles! We must use our words not to tear down but to call out the impossible in our marriages as we pray and intercede for our husbands. When we do this, we notice the fire that causes the hot air balloon to fly gets stronger and the hot air balloon begins soaring higher and stronger! As we agree with what God says about our husbands, despite what we see, we get to witness the transformation God has for them and it becomes a blessing and a miracle—and God uses US, the wives, the lifesavers, to take part in this amazing miracle!

Another beautiful part of this picture of the hot air balloon is that as we build up our husbands and our marriage, we realize it is a blessing to us as well! We are both in the hot air balloon together, and as it soars, as we bless and pray for our husbands, we truly thrive in a soaring marriage as God intended!

Faith: God is able. God will. We allow the Holy Spirit to call out the impossible in or marriage as we pray and intercede for our husbands. As we agree with what God says about our husbands, despite what we see, we get to witness the transformation God has for them, and it becomes a blessing and a miracle we take part in and benefit from.

2. You are to, above all else, _respect_ and be _submissive_ to your husband (Ephesians 5:22–24, 33; Colossians 3:18; and Titus 2:5).

After the fall of Adam and Eve, God told Eve, "Your desire will be for your husband, and he shall rule over you" (Genesis 3:16b). God was saying that she would have a sinful and selfish desire to control Adam, to usurp the man's headship, and Adam would have a sinful desire to dominate and control Eve. How do we escape these sinful desires in our marriage, and live out the role God Himself has for us as His followers? The Christian wife must submit to Christ! (Ephesians 5:22)

"Submissive" is the Greek word *hupotasso*, which means to get under and lift up or to put in order. It's a military term, as in when a soldier lines up in formation under a commanding officer. It is not a demeaning term that minimizes the soldier; it is a term that recognizes both roles as they relate to others in the military formation.

> **LEADER:** A little more on this word *hupotasso*: This is not the same as *obey*, which means to "follow a command." This is more of the idea of "yielding out of respect." Jesus as a child submitted to His parents (Luke 2:51); the demons submitted to the disciples when they went on their missionary tour (Luke 10:17); we are told to submit to governing bodies (Romans 13:1); ultimately all things will submit to the authority of Jesus (1 Corinthians 15:27). The wife who submits to her husband is giving a positive response to God who ordained the roles in marriage, even as a husband loves his wife sacrificially in following the example of Jesus.

What does it look like to respect your husband? Does your love for God lead you in your role as wife?

As stated with the husband, though the husband and wife are equal in their standing before God, in order for the family to function in harmony, the woman, with no loss of dignity, takes the place of submission to the headship of her husband.

Discuss 1 Corinthians 11:3. Does this mean Christ is inferior to God?

> **LEADER:** Of course, Christ is not inferior to God the Father, but as Philippians 2:4–8 states, Jesus willingly submitted Himself to the Father's will for our salvation.

When the woman seeks to usurp this authority and rule the home, havoc results and the home is left wide open for spiritual attack (Isaiah 3:12).

Our husbands are a spiritual covering for us, like an umbrella that protects us from the rain. As long as we stay in the place of godly submission, we are protected from needless spiritual attacks the enemy wants to "rain down on us." However, if we choose to usurp our husband's authority and rule the home ourselves, havoc results and we are left open for spiritual attack and so is our home.

> Thought: Submission is easier if we as wives feel secure and loved. This is God's plan.

3. Your role as wife is _evangelistic_ (1 Peter 3:1–2).

> LEADER: Although this passage is specifically for wives with unsaved husbands, the Christian wife shows the good news in Jesus to her Christian husband by her lifestyle in the same way.

Does this role of the wife depend on the behavior of the husband?

_____

_____

_____

_____

_____

Julie's Story

When John and I were first married, I truly thought I was a submissive wife. But I came to realize just how easy it is to fall into subtle forms of manipulation and control. I sometimes see things John doesn't see, which can be frustrating. But when that happened, I wasn't always honoring or respectful toward him. And if we are honest, it is easy for us as wives to make our husbands feel like idiots if we are not careful.

I cannot control my husband's decisions and at the same time expect him to be in the role that God called him to be as the leader of the home. I have to focus on my role as a wife and trust the Lord to work in my husband's life. It is my role to pray for him, respect him, and watch God move! The incredible thing is that as we continue to grow on this journey, I have seen God do miracles and real transformation. Staying focused on God and His purposes will bring us to an evangelical focus, taking us back to the gospel. And nothing is as transformational as watching the gospel take place in our marriage.

Even when the husband is unsaved or saved and not walking with the Lord, when we as wives choose to align with God's plan of submission, the Lord will deal with our husbands in His time and in His way!

Wives are called to submit to the headship of their husband, and husbands are to submit to the headship of Christ and love their wives as Christ loved the church. The issue is not superiority or inferiority. It is about God's order in the home. Most important, it is about obedience to God! (Philippians 2:1–4)

4. Your role is a position of _strength_ and _honor_ in God's kingdom (Romans 12:1–2).

Discuss how a wife displays her strength in God's eyes. How does this compare to what the world tells us?

_____

_____

_____

_____

_____

Discuss how our emotions as a wife can be used for good or evil. How does God want us to control our God-given gift of emotions?

_____

_____

_____

_____

5. You have the power to tear down your _house_ (Proverbs 14:1; 21:19; 31:18; 31:10). As wives you are made by God to be a source, through the power of the Holy Spirit, of nurturing love in the home, and you are priceless.

LEADER: Imagine when you were first married you saw your husband like this fence post—solid, dependable, and stable. Wives want a strong man we can lean on at times. We were created for that. But over the years, when you're constantly pushing back against him, wanting to

be in control, wanting your way, over time the fence post begins to move, to lean. Add years to that, a couple or three kids, and all the pressures of life. What happens? The fence post gets weaker and less stable. But the more we allow him the ability to figure things out and to lead, it has the opposite effect. It's like putting more cement around the fence post as you speak life to your husband—pray, edify, and speak encouraging words.

What can a wife do to build up or tear down her husband? Are her motives always inherently evil?

_____

_____

_____

_____

_____

6. It is a daily walk born out of a heart and love for God (Psalm 37:4; John 14:15).

Discuss how love for God motivates you to follow His Word. Will your affections follow?

LEADER: As you conclude, encourage wives to see how although our heart is really in the right place, we still bring harm but seeing our role as the one who constantly points out our husband's flaws and weaknesses. Instead, when we lay down our control and believe God is going to do something in our husbands, our marriages will soar, even with his flaws (and with yours!). It's not your job to be his flaw-noter. You are called to show him respect, which will make him thrive and more open to God's correction in his life. That's God's job. Be free from trying to fix your husband and trust the Lord.

Take-Home Discussion

Discuss with your husband:

1. What you do to make him feel respected, and what you do to make him feel disrespected.

_____

_____

_____

_____

_____

2. How unconditional love and unconditional respect/submission are born out of a love for God. How is it possible for you to perform your role as husband/wife (Ephesians 5:33)?

_____

_____

_____

_____

_____

3. How you both can extend grace/mercy/forgiveness when one stumbles in performing their role. Discuss how communication/openness can help you learn and be intentional (Colossians 3:13).

_____

_____

_____

_____

4. How God's plan for marriage works best when both are walking with God and making intentional efforts in performing their roles to unconditional love/respect (Galatians 5:16).

_____

_____

_____

_____

5. How important is it that you agree to pray together daily and agree to follow God's design for your marriage? Discuss how unity in marriage is only possible when you both agree to do marriage God's way (Matthew 7:24–27).

_____

_____

_____

_____

COMMUNICATION: THE NUMBER-ONE PROBLEM IN MARRIAGE

Ephesians 4:29

> **LEADER:** Take a few minutes to discuss the take-home assignment for the wives. Explain to the couples that the take-home work for husbands and wives highlights the importance of communication (or the need of it!).

Communication is said to be the number one problem in marriage. Through Scripture, we know that "death and life are in the power of the tongue" (Proverbs 18:21). In Ephesians 5:4, Paul tells us that there must be "no [none, zero] filthiness" in our speech. This means that when we talk, there is to be purity and love in our speech, and we should especially practice this in our marriage.

Our words have great power, especially in marriage. They should be gentle, ready to yield—not always insisting on your own way or your own viewpoint. Paul writes in Ephesians 4:29, "Let no corrupting talk come out of your mouths, but only such as is good for building up, as fits the occasion, that it may give grace to those who hear." The word translated "corrupting" in this passage actually means "rotting" or "decaying."[54] In Genesis 2:24, we see it is God's desire is for you to be one flesh spiritually, emotionally, and physically with your spouse. This bonding cannot happen without excellent communication skills. These skills have to be continually learned and refined.

Read the following:

- James 3:3–11
- Proverbs 10:19
- Matthew 12:34–36
- James 1:19

What are your main thoughts about communication after reading these?

_____

_____

_____

_____

_____

LEADER: These verses are critical for this lesson. Consider dividing the group into four small groups, giving each a passage to study. After a few minutes, let someone from each group read the passage and share their thoughts.

---

54 Harold W. Hoehner, "Ephesians" in *The Bible Knowledge Commentary: An Exposition of the Scriptures*, vol. 2, eds. John F. Walvoord, Roy B. Zuck (Wheaton, IL: Victor Books, 1985), 637.

As each passage is read and commented on, take a moment to point out how each would apply specifically to marriage. Encourage couples to respond with ways they might apply these words to their marriages. Remind them that we all fall short here and to see these verses and this lesson as an opportunity for growth.

You might note that when we first fall in love, we tend to be more careful with our words, but as we are married, over time we become comfortable with one another—which is a good thing—but we can become careless with our words. We can say things to our spouse in a tone of voice that we never would have when we were dating. Let this lesson be a place where we draw a line in the sand and commit to work together to communicate well.

Discuss how married believers should communicate. Do we sometimes fail to realize the power of the tongue to speak life or death?

_____

_____

_____

_____

_____

LEADER—ILLUSTRATION: Imagine I'm in my house with my family in the living room. I pick up a sword and start swinging it all over the place, around my kids and my wife. Suddenly, I nick

> my wife on the leg because I'm being careless with something
> that can bring harm.
>
> I could say, "I'm so sorry about that." But I made a wound
> there that will leave a scar. How many times do we speak words
> that can wound. We need to be very cautious with our words.
>
> As you pray together daily as a couple, asking God to guard
> your words is an important request.

There are three states in marriage:

Intimacy——Conflict——Withdrawal

A Christian marriage is a covenant between two followers
of Jesus under God's authority, but the two followers of Jesus are
still sinners. No matter how much you love one another, there are
times you will disagree, argue, and have conflict. Learning to face
these times of conflict in prayer to resolve them together will move
us from conflict back to intimacy. But when we fail to resolve a
conflict, it will lead us to withdraw from one another. One of the
most powerful ways to keep growing in your marriage is to learn
the simple line above and fight for each other to move conflict to
intimacy.

John and Julie's Story

Early in our marriage, we didn't see a lot of conflict in
our home. It was there; we just didn't perceive it. But as
our marriage continued, we started having more conflict
because everybody has conflict. That's part of the reality of
relationships.

As newlyweds, when we did notice conflict, we ran from it. We would have an argument; we wouldn't resolve it, and where did we go? To withdrawal, withdrawal that brought pain because we were made to live in intimacy. Intimacy is where you're going to be the most content and happy and feel so much joy and peace because you chose to resolve the conflict and not run from it. As we learned this concept as a couple, it changed our marriage, and it will change yours, too!

LEADER: This is one of the most important concepts in the curriculum, one that can help couples to grow and avoid deeper troubles down the road. It's simple, memorable, and powerful. Read the following or restate it to communicate the key ideas:

Intimacy is defined in Genesis 2:24 and the idea of "one flesh." Intimacy is oneness.

What happens when you have an argument or some conflict, and you move to resolve it together? What do you want to do? Touch each other, hold each other, and talk to each other. You want to be close.

But when you have an argument and you don't resolve it, what happens? The husband goes and turns on ESPN. But his wife may try to chase him around the house trying to resolve it.

ILLUSTRATION: Remember how Adam and Eve had perfect fellowship with God and with one another? Our hearts are still made for that, and we still long for that. We were made for this, and you can't change how you were created.

How do we transition from a state of conflict to a state of intimacy? Where do you want to live? Discuss the difficulty in remaining in a state of intimacy.

_____

_____

_____

_____

_____

How do we learn to get back to intimacy? Through communication. That's why communication is so important. We have to talk it out in ways that build each other up, not tear each other down. We fight for our marriage and for one another rather than fight against one another.

Suggestions for Excellent Communication

1. **Pray together daily.** Fight your battles on your knees. Give thanks in all circumstances and pray through your struggles. Pray first! (Matthew 15:18–19). Discuss the effect praying together has in your marriage communication.

> **LEADER:** Here is another place to emphasize again how vital prayer together daily is and to challenge couples who may have slipped in this daily commitment to renew it. Don't preach at them but remind them of the powerful benefit prayer is to their walk with God and their marriage. If they haven't found a consistent daily time to pray, urge them to do so this week.

2. **Pray** **before you have a difficult conversation** (1 Thessalonians 5:16–18; James 1:26; and Luke 6:45). Have a plan. Use Ephesians 5:25, 33 as a filter for your words to one another.

> **LEADER:** Remind couples of this perspective: Instead of looking at conflict with the mindset of "here we go again, another argument, another conflict," look at it like, "God wants to do something through this. He wants to grow us through this. He wants to transform us through this. He wants to help us conquer this together." So, when you have conflict and you resolve it, what happens to your marriage? You get more confident. You get stronger.
>
> How do you strengthen a muscle? Time under tension is one thing, and increasing volume is another. And there are more, like feeding yourself more protein, but you have to take your muscles through conflict for them to grow. Do you want a stronger marriage in ten years? Learn to move from conflict to intimacy rather than withdrawal by prayerfully communicating well.
>
> Your confidence grows when you have another conflict; resolve it with the help of the Holy Spirit and grow more. Conversely, what happens when you have a conflict, and you don't resolve it? You go to withdrawal. Like a person who never exercises and eats junk food, you get weaker, less healthy.

Discuss how communication in your home growing up affects the way you communicate now. How important it is to agree to the Lord's standard (Ephesians 4:29)? Unless you are intentional, you will likely do the same.

LEADER: Couples can show more grace and patience as they learn over time how communicating was modeled as they grew up. Examples:

- Some families never deal with conflict, which means their children may not realize either (1) the aversion they have to facing conflict, or (2) they overreact and want to face and resolve conflict immediately.
- Some families (or one of two parents) openly communicate affection and care, making it safe to see things differently, but other families (or one parent) communicate little to no affection, or in some cases respond to conflict with anger and selfishness.
- Share other examples/testimonies if you can.

Understanding what is already in your background to see why you communicate the way you do and why you perceive conflict the way you do is important. But here's the good news: knowing that you have a filter—a way of dealing with conflict—already, even if it has some flaws, means God can change your filter to His ideal.

Our background is part of us, but it does not have to rule us. No matter what your background or childhood was, you can learn to see marriage God's way and communicate from the foundation of spiritual health. God redeems and restores. You can have hope for now and the future from God's vantage point.

3. Learn and commit to good communication skills ! Timing is crucial: don't have a difficult discussion when either one of you is tired, stressed, or hurting (Proverbs 12:18; 25:11; and Galatians 5:15). It's not always what you say but how you say it.

Starbucks Moment

> **LEADER:** The "Starbucks moment" is vital here: the weekly time to get together when you aren't stressed, tired, or hurt. This keeps things from building up over time.

> **ILLUSTRATION:** Bricks: Imagine you have an argument over something trivial, like having two opinions on which route to take to go somewhere (like going to worship at church!). You don't resolve it, in part because it's not a big deal. But ignoring a conflict over time is like laying down a brick between you. One brick is no big deal. Another argument over the thermostat setting in the house (or an example of your choice) brings a brick, and then something else adds another. Nothing is huge, but over years this will build a wall to the ceiling, making it hard for you to see each other anymore.

4. Do not let Satan get a foothold (Ephesians 4:26–27).

> **LEADER:** Fighting for your marriage is a key part of spiritual warfare. Spiritual intimacy is vital here because the more we're bonded together spiritually, the better equipped we will be to walk through inevitable conflicts, giving us the strength to overcome temptation to blame each other and walk toward intimacy.
>
> It helps to keep in our minds God's ideal for marriage: to draw us out of ourselves, to move from selfishness and pride because He intended for us to have something greater.
>
> Some of our greatest victories and our greatest times in

> marriage can happen when we walk through conflict and resolve it. Just as people with a deep desire for health will push themselves to win in their workouts and diet, we can see conflict is an opportunity for growth.

Discuss the importance of having ground rules for communication (Colossians 4:6).

Four toxic traits to avoid. As the leader discusses the following toxic traits with the group, use the space to record your own thoughts about them.

Criticism

_____

_____

_____

_____

_____

Contempt

_____

_____

_____

_____

_____

Defensiveness

_____

_____

_____

_____

_____

Stonewalling

_____

_____

_____

_____

_____

LEADER: You can unpack these four important ideas more. However, you can also lovingly share that any couple who sees these as dominating their marriage could be helped by good and godly counseling. Also make yourself available (and any pastor/ staff) for couples to have confidential sessions to help. Remind them they are not alone.

1. *Criticism* is never productive, often happening when words like "always" or "never" come up often, but they really aren't true. "You never text me back/call me back." Well, unless you can show that they actually never do

so a single time, you've just been critical, which is not helpful.

2. *Contempt* is disrespectful. It's like rolling eyes at your spouse or slamming doors when you leave a room.

3. *Defensiveness* takes criticism and makes it painfully personal, like when one of you says, "I never do anything wrong. It's always you." You become defensive when you won't take personal responsibility. If defensiveness is taken to the extreme, you can have narcissistic behavior, gaslighting, and other things that do nothing but harm your marriage.

4. *Stonewalling* is when one of you refuses to say anything. The husband might say, "I'm going to watch ESPN." The wife might go into the bedroom and just avoid him for hours.

We want to avoid these things that are like the four horsemen of the communication apocalypse.

5. Remove the _fig_ _leaf_ (Genesis 2:25; 3:7). Be completely honest about how you feel about your needs, desires, dreams, and wants. This requires deep emotional transparency. Don't allow any subject in your marriage to be off-limits.

LEADER: This goes back to Adam and Eve and Genesis 2:25 where we read how they were created to be naked and unashamed. That means you were created to be one and open and transparent spiritually, emotionally, and physically. In Genesis 3:7, the first thing they did when they sinned was to cover themselves. You want to say, "Here I am," and have open, honest communication.

Never assume your spouse knows your needs or expectations. Remember men and women are different. Don't be frustrated or disappointed if your spouse doesn't completely understand your expectations. Subtle hints do not work (especially for guys!) (Proverbs 13:12).

> **LEADER:** Most, if not all, couples in the group will get that guys don't get subtle hints. Encourage the wives to say to their husbands: "Here's what I'm saying. What are you hearing?" And let their husbands repeat back what they said so you can really see what's resonating.

If you do not communicate your feelings, desires, thoughts to one another, do they simply just go away? Do you have to continually learn how to communicate as one? How do you balance Ephesians 4:29 and Genesis 2:25?

_____

_____

_____

_____

_____

6. Women communicate _three_ times more than men. Conversation to a woman is like _sex_ to a man.

> **LEADER:** This is not 100 percent the case for every woman or man but is true most of the time. A man desires physical

intimacy, and a woman desires emotional intimacy. For both of you, the starting place is your spiritual intimacy. The greater your spiritual connections, the greater your emotional connection. The greater your emotional connection, the greater your physical connection. Then, greater physical connection will lead to a greater spiritual connection. It's like a cycle.

Discuss types of communication together. Be proactive and intentional. The goal is proactive, not radioactive communication.

LEADER: Radioactive communication happens when you have an issue you can't ever talk about, or if it does come up, it blows up. It's a radioactive topic. Remember, men and women are different. Don't be frustrated or disappointed because your spouse doesn't completely understand your expectations.

7. **Request, inform but do not __nag__.** Only God can change your spouse. Prayer and your actions are powerful, not your words (Proverbs 21:19; 27:15; and 1 Peter 3:1–2).

Discuss the difference between deep communication and nagging.

LEADER: Nagging happens when you repeat the same request or say it with a harsh tone. Effective communication means paying attention to whether or not your spouse is focused on what you are saying and understanding that how your spouse hears what you say is more important than how you say it. "It's not what you say, it's what people hear."[55]

---

55 Frank Luntz, *Words That Work: It's Not What You Say, It's What People Hear* (New York: Hachette, 2008).

8. **Toxic communication can be a _heart_ problem** (Luke 6:45; Psalm 19:14; and Romans 8:6). Pray for/with one another.

Discuss how to change toxic/unloving/disrespectful communication in marriage.

9. **_Extend_ mercy and grace to one another.** Pursue unity in your communication (1 Corinthians 1:10; Colossians 3:13–14).

Discuss the gift of learning, growing, discovering unity and love in your communication. Agree to persevere together to strive for intimacy and not give up. You will be tempted to settle for withdrawal in exchange for temporary peace (Galatians 6:9).

Your willingness to grow together in your communication will set you up for success as you enter and progress through marriage. Be patient with one another and be willing to forgive.

Resist the urge to place a wall around yourself when hurt. Be completely honest with one another when hurting after a careless word. Trust the Lord and allow Him to direct you in your marriage. His refining in marriage is for your good and the good of your spouse. Pray over your communication together. Love God and love one another in word and deed.

> **LEADER:** This curriculum will help most couples to work through conflict and to return to intimacy. However, there may some instances where a couple comes to you in crisis and would be best served by meeting with a pastor or a Christian counselor to help them. Encourage any couples who seek this help by reminding them that seeking help from a pastor or counselor is not a sign of weakness or failure but shows a desire for a healthy marriage.

Review and Application

1. Discuss how you observed your parents communicate. Loud? Silent? Sarcasm?

_____

_____

_____

_____

_____

2. How do you want to communicate in your family? You are building a foundation now.

_____

_____

_____

_____

3. Discuss how you can have more proactive discussion and less reactive and radioactive discussions.

_____

_____

_____

_____

_____

4. Is there a radioactive topic in your marriage? How do you change that?

_____

_____

_____

_____

_____

5. Do you have a regular "Starbucks moment"? Intentionality?

_____

_____

_____

_____

6. What tendencies do you have in your communication when conflict arises?

_____

_____

_____

_____

_____

7. Discuss the importance of excellent communication to stay in a marital state of intimacy.

_____

_____

_____

_____

_____

8. Discuss how you two will move from a state of conflict/withdrawal to a state of intimacy.

_____

_____

_____

_____

_____

COMMUNICATION: MARRIAGE, FORGIVENESS, AND OFFENSE, PART 1

Colossians 3:12–14; 1 Corinthians 13:1; Proverbs 19:11

One of the true blessings in the life of a married believer is the opportunity to be one with the man or woman of your dreams. You will have many moments to love and enjoy the blessing God has given you in your spouse. Through the years, God desires you to enjoy the fruit in the wonderful journey of becoming one. This is truly a blessing, but it will only be possible for those who learn how to forgive and not take offense for the hurt and pain that is inevitable in the marriage covenant. Your spouse will make mistakes, disappoint you, hurt you, and let you down. God will give you the opportunity in your marriage to love as He loves, forgive as He forgives, and live in freedom if you obey Him and have faith in His way and Word. It is your choice—to live as the world lives or to live the life God has created you to experience, to live out the gospel of Jesus Christ.

This is especially true of the marriage covenant. Will you choose to forgive and love as Christ or pick and choose what commands you will follow? Your answer will impact the future of your life and marriage.

We live in a culture today marked by being offended and easily triggered. List some examples of this:

_____

_____

_____

_____

_____

LEADER: Write the responses on the board. Remind couples that any couple who has been married for long has stories of conflict. When we look back at some of them, we may laugh at how silly we acted: screaming, slamming doors, leaving the house in a huff, and basically acting just like seventh graders. We can react that way when we're in conflict because it's painful, and we don't know how to fix it. We are going to see specific ways to face and overcome conflict.

Discuss again the three states of marriage.

Intimacy——Conflict——Withdrawal

Read Genesis 2:24–25; Matthew 19:5; and Ephesians 5:31.

1. God _created_ you to be one—to be known and loved completely and unconditionally.

Discuss the fruit of your marriage when you are united as one and in a state of relational intimacy. Have you experienced God's perfect plan of oneness in your marriage? Describe how it feels. Have you experienced withdrawal? How does that feel? It is impossible to live as one if you do not forgive.

2. An offense is unforgiveness that will result in separation, pain, and _isolation_ if not handled correctly.

> **LEADER:** Here is a place where you can remind couples how they should expect good things in marriage as believers because we know that God is God and God is good. He gives good gifts to His children. His design for marriage when He created it was good and in response to Adam being alone and things were not good.
>
> But it is also true that we are sinners and imperfect, so we will sometimes do or say things that offend our spouses. Most of the time this is unintentional, but we especially have to guard against those times when we want to say or do something we know will offend because we are mad, hurt, or feel unappreciated.

Offense is more than just being angry, hurt, and disappointed. You can't be in a relationship with anyone in a meaningful way without at times experiencing these. Offense is *holding onto* the hurt, *nursing* bitterness, and allowing the wrong to *harden* your heart and contaminate your emotions and thinking. An offense is allowing pride and unforgiveness to reign in your life. The word *offense* is the Greek word *skandalon*, which is the trigger of a hunter's trap that holds the bait. Taking up an offense is dangerous because it makes the person who is offended blind to the other person's positive qualities and focus on their negative traits. You make a mental list of all the ways he or she has hurt or disappointed you. And, if you are offended enough, it will cause you to vilify them in every way.

Offense will also cause you to accentuate your good traits and focus on how you deserve better. It will also blind you to your own sin, which is pride. Offense creates division, lack of trust, and self-imposed isolation. This isolation only leads to more pain and distortion of truth. You eventually end up far away from God and other relationships. You build up walls and keep people at an emotional distance so you will never be hurt again.

Read Colossians 3:12–14.

> **LEADER:** Ask the group to name the various ways we are to act toward others from these three verses. After listing them, note how powerful these are when applied to a marriage.

LEADER

Deeper in the Word

Colossians 3:12–14

Background

Colossians 3 deals with practical matters that should mark believers' lives. Using the analogy of taking off and putting on clothes (vv. 8, 9, 10, 12, 14), Paul describes how the believer should look differently from those outside the faith. After spending the first two chapters on our identity in Christ, Paul next shows how we should look so that our new life is reflected in what we no longer "wear" and instead on how we choose to clothe ourselves as believers.

In verses 12–14, Paul addresses relationships within the church, which also applies to Christian couples. Verses 5–9 focus on what should be removed from our lives that is inconsistent with new life in Christ; beginning in verse 12, Paul gives positive features that should mark the Christian.

Supporting passages: Ephesians 3:14–19; 1 Peter 2:9–10.

Investigation

Verse 12: "Put on then." Now that Paul has explained what the "garments" of the believer should not include (vv. 5–9: specifically, anger, rage, malice, slander, filthy language, and lying), he turns to what should be apparent in a believer's life. Before listing those characteristics, he first reminds them of their identity. This is a crucial point: sometimes we can focus on what we are doing so much that we forget who we are. Who comes before what for the believer. Who are we in this verse? We are three things:

"Chosen ones." Chosen speaks to how much we are loved and desired by God. In contrast to those who display despicable traits (vv. 8–9), God's people are set apart for a different life.

"Holy." We are declared holy (set apart to God) at salvation. It is who we are but also a process by which we grow (sanctification).

"Beloved." We are saved by the sheer, unmatched love of God seen clearly in Jesus's death for us (Romans 5:8).

Paul then offers five appropriate garments for believers to wear to display their identity.

"Compassionate hearts." This term means "heartfelt sympathy for those suffering or in need."[56] The same term was used of Jesus when He saw the crowds and was moved with compassion (Matthew 9:36).

"Kindness." Compassion is the perspective to wear, and kindness is enacting it toward others, meeting the needs of others through good deeds.

"Humility." The "proper estimation of oneself (Rom 12:3) . . . not a self-debasing attitude (like the 'false humility' of 2:18 and 2:23) but an attitude that is free from pride and self-assertion."[57]

"Meekness" or **"gentleness."** It is "the opposite of self-interest and reveals itself in gentleness. It is a spirit of quiet submission, not weakness but rather a spirit of Christian courtesy."[58]

"Patience" or **"self-restraint."** It's important to remember that just because someone invites you to an argument or a fight, you don't have to join.

Verse 13: Paul follows these five marks with two related ideas: enduring and forgiving.

---

56 Max Anders, *Galatians, Ephesians, Philippians & Colossians,* Holman New Testament Commentary (Nashville: Broadman & Holman, 1999), 331.

57 Anders, *Galatians, Ephesians, Philippians & Colossians,* 331.

58 Ian McNaughton, *Opening Up Colossians and Philemon* (Leominster, MA: Day One, 2006), 64–66.

"Bearing with one another." First, enduring or forbearing. This is the response a believer should take rather than being easily offended. Very literally it is "holding yourselves back from one another."[59] In our day marked by outrage, polarization, and offense, it is especially vital for married couples to practice this together.

"If one has a complaint ... forgiving." The word for "complaint" is found only here in the New Testament and has the idea of comparison. A popular aphorism observes that comparison is the thief of joy. This is especially truth for married couples!

"As the Lord has forgiven you, so you also must forgive." "Anyone can hold grudges, but the mark of Christians is that they do not. They forgive regardless. The pattern for this behavior is Christ's forgiving the believer. The term used here for forgiveness, charizomai, is the same that occurs in the command to the believer."[60]

Verse 14: "Above all these put on love." Love is supreme. Paul saves the best clothing for last and gives two qualifications here to show why love is supreme. First, love is above all. The word is *agape*, which is used to describe God's love. Paul beautifully comments on this love in 1 Corinthians 13.

"Which binds everything together in perfect harmony." It is the one thing that, to use Paul's analogy, brings together the wardrobe to display God's work of grace in a person. "Christian

---

59 Richard R. Melick, *Philippians, Colossians, Philemon*, The New American Commentary, vol. 32 (Nashville: Broadman & Holman, 1991), 300.

60 Melick, *Philippians, Colossians, Philemon*, 300.

love is above all these other important and beautiful graces because it is self-sacrificing, self-giving, and the fulfilment of both the law and the gospel. It is a new commandment given to us by our Saviour (John 13:34–35). The local church needs lashings of love for unity to be maintained."[61]

Importance

This passage reminds believers—and Christian couples—to be grounded in our identity and to wear garments that reflect that identity as we interact with one another and the world.

> The Christian wardrobe contains garments that were bought by Christ when he died on the cross. This collection of spiritual apparel, tailored by his Spirit, needs to be searched daily in order that garments appropriate for the moment are chosen and worn. The resulting "new look" and behaviour will bring praise and acclaim to the head of the church. With this holy fashion, new behaviour will display the believer's new life in Christ. The new wardrobe is not for special occasions only, but for everyday use, and when it is put on it also "feels" good.[62]

Hans Christian Andersen's story "The Emperor's New Clothes" reminds believers not to take off our old clothes without putting more suitable clothes back on. We are all wearing "garments" that reflect our lives.

This offers vital wisdom for Christian marriages. A couple who walks with Jesus should remember daily who they are in

---

61 McNaughton, *Opening Up Colossians and Philemon*, 66–67.
62 McNaughton, *Opening Up Colossians and Philemon*, 66.

Christ. Their standing before God is *chosen, holy,* and *beloved.* God desires a relationship with both husband and wife and with the two as a couple. He chose believers to be His special people. He calls believers to a life of holiness, and He reminds believers of the status they enjoy.

No matter what conflict or circumstances you face in your marriage, you can rest with the assurance that God called you to be His own, that you can be holy, and that you are loved by Him. And as Paul said of the chosen (Romans 8:33), *nothing* can separate you from that love (Romans 8:38–39). We do not serve a capricious God who is looking for reasons to condemn; we are children to a compassionate God who is slow to anger and abounding in love (Psalm 103:8). It is from this identity that Christian couples can face the challenges of living for Jesus in this broken world.

When we know who we are in Christ, we can face each day wearing the garments that represent that identity. We can wear the fashion of our King: kindness, humility, meekness, patience, and expressing forgiveness to one another, remembering that we will never forgive to the level that Christ forgave us in salvation.

Implications

Olympic Gold Medalist Dan Jansen's sister Jane died from leukemia prior to the 1988 Winter Games in Calgary. He skated for gold in honor of his sister but failed in Calgary and in the 1992 games in Albertville. But in Lillehammer, Norway, in 1994, he set a world record, winning the gold in the 1,000 meters. As he skated his victory lap, he held his nine-month-old daughter named Jane in his arms.

He was asked how he endured for so many years. He mentioned a conversation with his father after a meet he lost when he was twelve. Dan was pouting all the way home; his father was quiet. As Dan headed to bed that night, his dad came to his bedside and made a statement that changed his perspective. "Son," he said, "life is more than skating in circles."[63]

That statement gave Dan a bigger perspective on life. Sometimes it may seem that a marriage is just going in circles, in a rut. Communication issues often get a couple into that place, and better communication can help move out of it.

Dealing with issues like this from the perspective of our identity in Christ is a better way to start. Reflecting on the values Paul gives here can help bring humility, forgiveness, and a renewed love.

One more thing: in verse 15, Paul says to be thankful. Expressing gratitude has proven to be one of the most powerful ways to shift our mindset. It is very difficult to be upset with someone while at the same time expressing gratitude for them.

As followers of Jesus, we all want to honor Him. But we still sin in this life and fail the Lord and others. We need His help to display the marks noted in these verses. How do we handle hurt so that we can forgive, move back to intimacy, and not take offense?

_____

_____

_____

---

63 Anders, *Galatians, Ephesians, Philippians & Colossians*, 331.

3. __Stop__ and go immediately to God in prayer (Colossians 3:12–14). Remember most offenses are not intentional, but the hurt is real and must be addressed in a productive, loving way. Apply Romans 12:1–2; 2 Corinthians 10:5; and 1 Corinthians 13:1.

A 1999 study of 124 newlywed couples by researchers John Gottmann and Sybil Carrère with the University of Washington found that how each spouse shared and responded to conflict in the first three minutes is a strong indicator in whether or not the couple will divorce.[64]

For instance, 80 percent of the time the wife initiates the issue and does so in the form of a general criticism that impugns the husband's character rather than emphasizing the specific issue. The husband then responds defensively. Of the seventeen couples who later divorced, they all began with much greater displays of negative emotion and fewer positive words. Stable couples gave more positive comments, and husbands did not initially respond with defensiveness. Starting with prayer and asking God to help can calm you both and seek a positive resolution.

LEADER: Here is more from the study you could share:

Drs. Carrère and Gottman found that the startup of the conflict discussion was key to predicting divorce or

---

64 Ellie Lisitsa, "Predicting Divorce from the First 3 Minutes of Conflict Discussion," The Gottman Institute, https://www.gottman.com/blog/the-research-predicting-divorce-among-newlyweds-from-the-first-three-minutes-of-a-marital-conflict-discussion/.

> marital stability. As noted above, of the 17 couples who later divorced, **all** started off their conflict discussions with significantly greater displays of negative emotion and fewer expressions of positive emotion when compared with couples who remained married over the course of the 6-year study. In stable marriages, both husbands and wives expressed less negative affect and more positive affect at the first three minutes of such discussions.
>
> Dr. Gottman on his 6-year study: "The biggest lesson to be learned from this study is that the way couples begin a discussion about a problem—how you present an issue and how your partner responds to you—is absolutely critical."[65]

Why does an offense from your spouse hurt more than from others? Love requires sacrifice and vulnerability.

_____

_____

_____

_____

_____

How do you go to God when you have encountered an offense?

_____

_____

_____

---

65 Lisitsa, "Predicting Divorce from the First 3 Minutes of Conflict Discussion."

How do forgiveness and resolution lead you back to oneness? Discuss the three states of marriage.

What will happen in your marriage if you don't forgive?

How do you know if you have taken an offense?

Read:

- Luke 17:4–5
- Matthew 5:3–5, 7–9, 23–24, 44–48
- Matthew 7:3–5

How do these verses help us see the importance of forgiveness and not allowing unforgiveness to build up over time?

_____

_____

_____

_____

_____

LEADER: For these verses, you could divide the group up into four small groups and assign the following: group 1, Luke 17:4–5; group 2, Matthew 5:3–5, 7–9; group 3, Matthew 5:23–24, 44–48; group 4, Matthew 7:3–5. Give them a few minutes, then let each group share their responses with the whole group.

Review and Application

1. As a couple, can you identify areas that more easily create conflict in your marriage (it could be a habit, an attitude, an action, or failing to do something your spouse considers important)?

_____

_____

2. How can developing the marks seen in Colossians 3:12–14 help you as a couple to fight for each other and for intimacy rather than moving toward withdrawal?

3. Why do you think it is easier for us to want grace shown to us than to extend it to someone else? How can you work on extending mercy and grace to your spouse?

COMMUNICATION: MARRIAGE, FORGIVENESS, AND OFFENSE, PART 2

Colossians 3:12–14; 1 Corinthians 13:1; Proverbs 19:11

Remember the three states of marriage:

Intimacy——Conflict——Withdrawal

Read again Colossians 3:12–14.

How do we handle hurt so that we can forgive, move back to intimacy, and not take offense?

Last week we learned the first response:

1. **Stop** **and go immediately to God in prayer.**

Here are more responses:

2. **Guard** **your heart and mouth** (Proverbs 4:23; 18:21; Psalm 51:10; Matthew 12:34).

Story from John and Julie

John: Recently, we were in the car and were having a good time. It was just the two of us on a beautiful day. The top was down; the air felt great. It was one of those glorious days. And Julie said, "You know, you don't reach out and hold my hand anymore." I was thinking about how I was really enjoying the drive and suddenly she brought that up. I could have replied, "What are you talking about? You just spoiled a really good drive." But on this occasion, I heeded this point and guarded my heart and mouth. What did I do? I reached over and took her hand.

Julie: Yes, he did!

John: I realized that I love holding her hand. So, instead of being defensive, I reached for her hand, and I've been doing it more since then.

Julie: And I noticed.

The beautiful part about communication issues is when you can say, "Hey, you never reach for my hand," and instead of being met with defensiveness, your spouse responds lovingly.

GROUP DISCUSSION

What does it mean to guard your heart above all else?

_____

_____

_____

_____

LEADER: Explain an unintended consequence of living in withdrawal and refusing to deal with conflict or offense: you can lose confidence in God. You must guard your heart here as well to be aware of developing resentment or doubt toward the Lord. Remember that after Adam and Eve sinned, Adam pointed to Eve but really implicated God when he said, "The woman whom **you gave** to be with **me, she gave** me the fruit" (Genesis 3:12, author's emphasis). Take personal responsibility. Let your love for God lead you to forgive like He has forgiven you.

How do you guard your heart against unforgiveness?

_____

_____

_____

_____

How difficult is it to guard your mouth when you're hurt? (*Hint:* go to God first.)

_____

_____

_____

_____

_____

3. _Share_ your feelings with your spouse after you have gone to God in prayer (Genesis 2:24–25; Proverbs 13:12).

LEADER: Here's encouragement for couples struggling with pain and offense. Did you know that almost half (sixty-five) of the Psalms are psalms of lament (see Psalms 44; 60; 79)?[66] David or someone else is crying out to God in pain, or sorrow, or fear because they believed the place to go when conflict comes is to God. These psalms are honest and raw. Almost all end up in praise to God, and you can see this in your marriage.

It's not unspiritual to stop and pray in a hard conflict, it's very spiritual to do so. Invite God into it: "God, come into this pain. Come into this withdrawal, come into this situation. We invite you in. Show us how to do this." For as you pray together, the issue moves from his side or her side to God's side. That's your goal for the communication.

How do you communicate your hurt to your spouse in a loving way?

_____

_____

_____

_____

_____

How does going to God first help in sharing your hurt to your spouse?

_____

_____

_____

---

66 Rob Brockman, "The Art of Lament," The Gospel Coalition, March 30, 2021, https://ca.thegospelcoalition.org/article/the-art-of-lament/.

_____

_____

_____

4. When your spouse is hurt from your actions, _listen_ and be humble (Proverbs 15:31–33; 17:9; Ephesians 4:1–5; James 1:1).

Should you ask for forgiveness even when you do not understand how your actions caused pain? Why?

_____

_____

_____

_____

_____

Is this a time for defensiveness and exaggeration?

_____

_____

_____

_____

Is James 5:16 an obvious part of your marriage?

_____

_____

_____

_____

_____

5. __Forgiveness__ **leads to freedom, oneness, and blessing** (Colossians 3:13; Ephesians 4:32; Matthew 6:14–15; 18:21–22; Mark 11:25).

> **LEADER:** Remind the group that no matter what is done to us and how hard it may seem to forgive, we will never forgive to the level God has forgiven us, and we will never offend anyone the way our sin offended God. Yet, God sent Jesus for our sin against Him to be forgiven!
>
> God is the God of new things, new starts, and new songs.
>
> When forgiveness seems hard, take some time to reflect. Focus not on the pain that you carry in this moment but on God's great love and forgiveness toward you. Think about God's goodness to you, the times He has clearly shown His care for you.

Does forgiveness mean approval?

_____

_____

_____

_____

_____

Does forgiveness always feel good?

_____

_____

_____

_____

_____

What do you feel like when you're forgiven?

_____

_____

_____

_____

_____

Compare and contrast the life of forgiveness and freedom versus unforgiveness and offense.

_____

_____

_____

_____

_____

6. **Pray** **together that God will help you both learn how to forgive completely and to never take up an offense** (2 Corinthians 10:5; James 1:25).

Take some time this week to reflect on Jesus, the cross, and how He showed such incredible forgiveness to us. Thank Him for that!

7. __Thank__ the Lord for His example of forgiveness and how to live a life of oneness and freedom (1 Thessalonians 5:16–18; 2 Corinthians 3:17; Luke 23:34; 1 John 1:7).

> **LEADER:** Stress the importance of GRATITUDE. One of the postures you want to develop is to choose gratitude consistently rather than negative attitudes. The weekly "Starbucks moment" offers a place to cultivate gratitude as a couple. Developing the posture of gratitude helps you to see the blessings even in hard things. For instance: "Yes, we need to work through this conflict, but I'm grateful that God is for us, and He desires for us to be intimate. I'm grateful you are here having this conversation. I'm grateful for all the ways our marriage is healthy and brings joy."
>
> Thank your spouse for being present with you. Thank him/her for going to work. If you find it difficult to be grateful for things in your marriage or your spouse, that's a good sign you are deep in withdrawal.
>
> Doing this keeps you or your spouse from dreading the facing of conflict or choosing to avoid it. It helps you to handle it in a way that is going to be life-giving.

The Christian marriage should model Christ and His bride, the church. This institution God created should display the gospel to the lost world on how to live and love as Christ. He taught and displayed how to love unconditionally, forgive completely, and live in freedom. The world and its ways will always cry and long for revenge, personal rights, and conditional love. The world cries out, "You will have to earn it, and the person will decide when and how to live, forgive, and love." This, in essence, is creating your own god for your interests. This will result in disunity, separation, and a self-created prison. In every relational failure among believers, one or both parties at some point choose not to forgive, leading to separation, disunity, and offense.

You as a married man/woman will have a decision to make: to live as Christ or settle for what the world offers (Galatians 2:20).

Review and Application

1. Discuss the results of unforgiveness and taking up an offense. Acknowledge the danger of offense.

_____

_____

_____

_____

_____

2. Discuss and share anything you need to ask your spouse for forgiveness.

_____

_____

_____

_____

_____

3. Pray together and ask the Lord to reveal any offense you have taken against your spouse or anyone else. Confess and forgive.

_____

_____

_____

_____

_____

4. Extend mercy and grace to one another and discuss how you want your marriage to forgive and to never take an offense.

_____

_____

_____

_____

_____

GREAT EXPECTATIONS, PART 1

Romans 8:28

We all have expectations of life and its direction. This is especially true of marriage. There are so many unanswered questions/expectations that wait to be discovered. This continual process is one of the true joys of life. Questions like: "How happy will we be; what kind of house and neighborhood will we live in; how many children will we have; how will we celebrate holidays; how much money will we have; I'm sure I'll stay home when our children are born; how successful will my career be (or my husband's); I'm sure my husband will always want to talk to me; we will always feel in love; I'm sure we will always want to have sex as much as I desire," and on and on and on. In fact, we all have expectations (maybe subconscious, unknown) about life and marriage. It's based on gender, upbringing, culture, etc. However, should we focus our expectations in marriage on something other than our wants/desires and happiness? Our expectations should be based in the word of God: His will and design for my life versus my will and design, His kingdom versus my kingdom. Have you surrendered your marriage to God? What do we do about unrealized expectations in our marriage? What are your expectations? Do you know? (Jeremiah 29:11; 1 Thessalonians 5:16–18; Proverbs 3:5; Hebrews 11:1)

LEADER: This lesson aims to reveal misplaced expectations while affirming expectations that are in line with God's purposes. One of the practical ways to help couples think about this is to focus less on expectations and more on appreciation: Instead of expecting the husband/wife to meet the kind of misplaced expectations given below, encourage them to give more attention to focusing on what they appreciate about their spouses. Once they view their spouses from a perspective of *appreciation*, they can focus on more appropriate *expectations* from God's Word.

Misplaced Expectations

Discuss unrealized, unspoken, subconscious expectations (Jeremiah 2:13).

See if you can identify with any of these when you think about the beginning of your marriage together:

1. I will always be __happy__ with my spouse, and I will always feel __loved__ .

2. My spouse will make me __whole__ . (Don't put your spouse where God belongs!)

3. Everything bad in our relationship will go away when we get __married__ , but everything good in our relationship will get better when we get married!

4. Husband: my wife will do things just like my __mother__ . Wife: my husband will do things just like my __father__ .

5. We will never __argue__ or disagree.

6. My spouse will never _hurt_ me, and I will never hurt my spouse.

7. I will always understand my _spouse_ .

8. As long as we love God and each other, marriage will always be _easy_ .

Discuss the potential danger/result of misplaced expectations apart from God. What are ways the world and its expectations of life/marriage affect you in your marriage? How do we overcome this?

_____

_____

_____

_____

_____

Divine Expectations: Isaiah 55:1–2

LEADER: Isaiah 55 is an amazing passage about the love and compassion of God. In verses 1–2 we see how God invites us to come to Him to be satisfied. This is a good place to remind couples that God is a giver of good things when we come to Him, and His ways are best.

You may want to read through verse 13. This is a passage of great hope for us and for our marriages. Notice that in verses 6–7 we see how God welcomes those who have been wicked to return to Him to find mercy and forgiveness because His thoughts are not our thoughts (v. 8). This is a great promise about divine expectations for discouraged couples.

1. You should expect God to honor your _prayer_ together daily to walk in the Spirit and develop spiritual unity in marriage (Matthew 18:20; 1 Thessalonians 5:16–18).

How does unity in marriage reflect your relationship with God?

_____

_____

_____

_____

_____

2. You should expect to work to have _intimacy_ with one another with God's help (Genesis 2:18; 2:24).

How is it possible to live in a state of intimacy in your marriage?

_____

_____

_____

_____

_____

LEADER: This is a good place to review Intimacy—— Conflict——Withdrawal.

3. Husbands should expect to practice tenderness and unconditional _love_ toward their wives, and wives should expect to practice unconditional _respect_ toward their husbands (Ephesians 5:25; Deuteronomy 24:5; Ephesians 5:33; 1 Peter 3:7).

How is possible for the husband to love as Christ loves? How is it possible for the wife to respect unconditionally?

_____

_____

_____

_____

_____

4. You should expect to strive to _leave_ and cleave (Genesis 2:24).

How is it possible to leave all and cleave together?

_____

_____

_____

_____

_____

5. You should expect to be totally _honest_ with your spouse (Colossians 3:9).

What is the result of partial or incomplete truth in marriage?

_____

_____

_____

_____

_____

6. You should expect to protect purity in your _physical_ _intimacy_ , remembering that your body is not yours _alone_ (Hebrews 13:4; Proverbs 4:23; 1 Corinthians 7:3–5; Genesis 1:28*a*).

> **LEADER:** In this context the 1 Corinthians 7 passage is especially important. God's desire for marriage is to experience consistent physical intimacy and sexual fulfillment in marriage. This passage does not teach that a spouse may demand sexual intimacy but elevates the importance of physical intimacy as a priority in marriage. As noted earlier, men typically value sexual intimacy more, while women tend to value conversation more.

How is it possible to maintain purity and physical intimacy in your marriage?

_____

_____

_____

_____

_____

7. The husband and wife should expect to know their _role_ (1 Corinthians 11:3; Ephesians 5:25, 33).

How will you know your role as husband or wife?

_____

_____

_____

_____

_____

8. You will be faithful (Exodus 20:14; Matthew 5:28).

How is it possible to be faithful?

_____

_____

_____

_____

Discuss the peace and unity in marriage when your expectations together as a married couple are in alignment with God. How difficult is it to surrender your will and expectations to God?

_____

_____

_____

_____

_____

Discuss how an agreement to follow God and His will in your life and marriage leads to unprecedented unity in your marriage.

_____

_____

_____

_____

_____

We, as believers, should expect to pursue unconditional love, support, and acceptance independently (Philippians 2:4).

Conclusion: My marriage will not be as I expect, and my response to that will determine my life and my relationship with God and my spouse. Try to focus on what you can give, not what you get. Homework: write down as many expectations as you can and share with your spouse openly.

Review and Application

1. What is your ideal picture of a husband? Wife?

_____

_____

_____

_____

_____

2. What is your plan when you don't get what you're expecting?

_____

_____

_____

_____

_____

_____

3. Discuss how you will deal with unspoken, unrealized expectations.

_____

_____

_____

_____

_____

4. What are some expectations you have regarding birthdays, anniversaries, Christmas, and other holidays?

_____

_____

_____

_____

_____

5. What are your expectations on how you will spend weekends, evenings, free time, and so on?

_____

_____

_____

_____

_____

6. Discuss your expectations regarding money: saving, spending, tithing.

_____

_____

_____

_____

_____

7. Discuss how deep, open, honest communication helps with your expectations.

_____

_____

_____

_____

_____

GREAT EXPECTATIONS, PART 2

Jeremiah 29:11

LEADER: Jeremiah 29 is a remarkable passage. You will see more in-depth material on verses 11–13 here, but you may want to begin this last week with a deeper look at verses 5–14, which is the first part of the letter from Jeremiah. Note how God's people—in exile in Babylon at this time—were told in verse 7 to work for the good of the people and the land of Babylon. In some ways today, it may seem like we as Christians are in a similar place as we live in a land that doesn't generally value marriage, the gospel, or other things of God. But we can by our healthy marriages and our walk with Christ. We can work for the good of our world as Jeremiah describes. As we surrender to the Lord to guide our marriages, it impacts others for His glory and their good!

LEADER

Deeper in the Word

Jeremiah 29:11–13

Background

Jeremiah 29 gives us the letter Jeremiah sent to Jews who were in Babylonian exile (vv. 1–14). False prophets had told the people they would soon return home; Jeremiah wrote to let them know they were in for a lengthy stay.

Speaking for the Lord, the prophet encouraged them to live in exile, to "build houses and live in them; plant gardens and eat their produce" (v. 5). He told them to marry and have families and, in terms of how they were to relate to the Babylonian people, to "seek the welfare of the city where I have sent you into exile, and pray to the LORD on its behalf, for in its welfare you will find your welfare" (v. 7). This chapter reminds believers how to live in our fallen world as we await the Lord's return. "Jeremiah wanted them to be good witnesses to the idolatrous Babylonians, and he also wanted them to be good Jews even though separated from their temple and its services."[67]

In the middle of the letter Jeremiah gives verses 11–13, some of the most familiar and beloved in the book of Jeremiah. It's important to remember that these verses were speaking to a specific time in history to God's people in a time of exile showing that although their sin led them to become exiles, God's grace and compassion was still at work. God would restore His people in due time.

These verses also speak to believers today as they echo key truths seen throughout the Bible. First, God is God—He is sovereignly ruling over history and our lives. Second, God is good, and restoration is a natural outflow of His grace. Third, God delights in fellowship with His children who seek Him. First, however, the consequences for their sin must be experienced, so their exile would last seventy years (v. 10).

---

67 Warren W. Wiersbe, *Be Decisive* (Wheaton, IL: Victor Books, 1996), 123.

Supporting passages: Matthew 6:33–34; Matthew 7:7–10; Proverbs 16:3, 9.

Investigation

The Lord assured the people that what had happened was not a series of unplanned, accidental events. He said in verse 11, "I know the plans" (lit. "I, I know" is emphatic in Hebrew). His plan was not intended to hurt them but to give them "a future and a hope." He encouraged them to pray, for He would listen to them. However, see 11:14 and 14:11, where He told Jeremiah not to pray, for He would not listen.

Verse 11: "For I know." God knows us. God knows our names, our strengths and weaknesses, all about us. God loves us and uses us for His glory, imperfect as we are. There is no doubt in God's mind that He has good for them. The false prophets Jeremiah faced did not know all things, but God is truly omniscient.

Restoration is a major theme in Scripture. Scholars summarize the Bible's entire scope with the four themes of Creation, Fall, Redemption, and Restoration. In this chapter, Jeremiah is speaking specifically of the restoration of Jews to their homeland, but the idea of restoration is found across the books of the Bible.

"The plans I have for you." God created us in His image to know and worship Him. We come to know Him through Jesus Christ, who saves us by grace through faith. The Spirit of God becomes our guide. God has a plan for your life. But so does Satan, as do other people, and so do you. It is not our job to create a plan that God will bless but to surrender to His plan for us.

God's plan is based on knowing Him and searching His Word, and His plan for you will be consistent with His Word. Each person is wired differently. That's why in marriage each spouse should not try to force the other to become something other than what God called them to be. God wires each person with their personality, gives spiritual gifts, and allows experiences in life to help shape us to be more like Jesus.

"Plans for welfare and not for evil." The term for "welfare" is shalom, or "peace," a term indicating well-being, wholeness, harmony, and peace. In the short term, it may seem that our struggles indicate God's lack of interest in us, but His silence is not to be confused with His inaction.

"To give you a future and a hope." This could be translated as "a future filled with hope." As long as God is involved, there is hope. No matter how dark the circumstances, if you are breathing and you know Jesus, you have hope. You have a future. Look at Peter for an example: Jesus called him the "rock" even though He, being God, knew Peter would deny Him (Matthew 16:18). And yet Peter, having been broken and in tears after his denial, was still used by God to preach at Pentecost, serve God in suffering (Acts 4, 12), and write the Epistles of 1 and 2 Peter.

Hope is one of the great marks of the Christian faith. Hope for the believer is not like that of the world. It's not a wish; it's a promise. "Hope is that part of faith that focuses on the future. In biblical terms, when faith is directed to the future, you can call it hope. But faith can focus on the past and the present too, so faith is the larger term."[68]

---

68 Elmer A. Martens, "Jeremiah," in Evangelical Commentary on the Bible, vol. 3 (Grand Rapids, MI: Baker Books, 1995), 540.

Peter talked about the "living hope" believers have that includes our future inheritance in heaven (1 Peter 1:3). There is no uncertainty about that hope coming into being for the believer!

Verse 12: "Then you will call upon me and come and pray to me." God's answer is not always immediate even when we are impatient. Prayer is foundational for the Christian and therefore is foundational for marriage. How do we find what God promised in verse 11, the hope and the future ahead, and our well-being? We call out to God in prayer.

Puritan Matthew Henry said this about verse 12: "When God is about to give his people the expected good he pours out a spirit of prayer, and it is a good sign that he is coming towards them in mercy."[69]

"And I will hear you." Prayer is less about geography (like being in Jerusalem) and more about proximity (being near to God). While physically separated from their land, "they can find him in intimate personal relationship in Babylon as in Jerusalem—without Temple, land, priests, sacrifice—if they seek him with all the energy of intellect and will."[70] It is also less about getting God to respond to us and helping us better hear from and respond to God. God does hear us, but the timing of His response is often on a different timetable than ours.

Verse 13: "You will seek me and find me." This is good news! God does not play Easter egg hunt or hide-and-seek with us. One

---

69 Matthew Henry, *Matthew Henry's Commentary on the Whole Bible: Complete and Unabridged in One Volume* (Peabody, MA: Hendrickson, 1994), 1285.

70 Leo J. Green, "Jeremiah," in *The Teacher's Bible Commentary*, ed. H. Franklin Paschall and Herschel H. Hobbs (Nashville: Broadman and Holman, 1972), 465.

of the great promises in Scripture is found here. The question is not whether God can be found but whether we are seeking Him.

This calls to mind Matthew 7:7 where Jesus teaches on persevering prayer by telling us to ask, seek, and knock.

"When you seek me with all your heart." We are to seek the Lord with all our hearts or more than anything else in life.

> Verse 13 is one of the great evangelistic texts of the OT (cf. Deut 4:29). It says God is accessible. If we seek him, we will find him when we want him more than all else ("with all your heart," i.e., with the mind, the will). God assured his people that when they sought him wholeheartedly, he would be found. He would then gather them from all nations where he had scattered them and bring them back from captivity after they repented (cf. Deut 30:1–5).[71]

Importance

One of the dangers of a wonderful, intimate relationship is taking the other person for granted. We can do that in our walk with God, taking for granted His faithfulness and grace. It's sad but true that most of the time a believer experiences great growth spiritually comes after recognizing an area of neglect or indifference over spiritual things. The Spirit of God convicts us, creating a desire to know and serve God more faithfully. When this happens to a larger group of people at the same time, we call it revival. But individual believers need that as well.

---

71 F. B. Huey, *Jeremiah, Lamentations*, vol. 16, The New American Commentary (Nashville: Broadman & Holman, 1993), 254.

The same is true in marriage. A wonderful, God-focused marriage can suffer when one spouse (or both) begins to take the other for granted. Or, one or both take their focus off continuing to grow in their relationship. Most serious is when one or both stop pursuing God with all their hearts. The Jews had done just this with the Lord. They took their focus off God and worship of Him, which opened the door for idols to enter. Eventually the nation, first Israel and then Judah, were judged by God and taken into captivity because of their idolatry.

And yet God, who is

> Gracious and compassionate,
>   slow to anger and abounding in love,
>   and he relents from sending calamity. (Joel 2:13 NIV)

continually moves to restore. He restored His people in the Old Testament. He can restore you. He can renew and restore your marriage.

Implications

When difficult times arise in marriage (and they will), remember God's words: He is for our welfare and not to harm us. He promises hope and a future. Restoration is always a possibility when God is involved.

It was God's plan that caused Israel and Judah to be in exile as judgment for their idolatry. A vital part of our own discipleship as believers and as a Christian couple is to believe that God may either allow us or sometimes even lead us into difficult seasons. There are several reasons for this.

First, we walk though difficulty as a consequence of our sin. This is what we see here with the Jews. Second, we suffer for a season because of God's loving discipline. Hebrews 12:6–11 reminds us that God disciplines those He loves. But He does not abandon us, nor did He abandon His people in exile. Third, we go through seasons of suffering to refine us, like gold is proven more valuable by fire (Proverbs 17:3). Fourth, we suffer simply as a result of a fallen world. We face disease, nations go to war, and we have strife in our own relationships because we are embedded in a world that is broken by sin (Romans 8:18–25). Finally, sometimes we suffer because of the cruelty or sin of others. Abuse, neglect, or persecution are all examples of this (Ephesians 4:31–32).

But no matter how suffering comes upon us or whether we fully understand its purpose in this life, we have the hope that God will bring restoration, either in this life or certainly in the next.

Jeremiah tells us that God has a perfect plan to provide and to bless us. However, during unexpected times in life, we are often tempted to wonder, "God, what are you doing here? This does not look like I thought it would." Your marriage is no different.

At every wedding, a man marries the woman he believes will be his ideal wife, and a woman marries the man she thinks will be her ideal husband. Then, as the pages of the calendar turn, they realize their spouse and marriage are not what they expected, and the result is disappointment. What actually happened, however, is they discovered the real person they married, and whether they realize it or not, that is a gift from God. This unsettling discovery can actually be good for a marriage if you learn how to unpack the discovery. Just as you surrendered your life to follow Christ, you will have to learn to surrender your spouse and marriage to God.

What are your thoughts on the above paragraph? Is it wrong to have high expectations?

_____

_____

_____

_____

_____

What are some common expectations for the wife? Husband? Where do these expectations come from? Do you think the differences in expectations will be cause for discouragement/conflict?

_____

_____

_____

_____

_____

What is an unspoken expectation? What is an unrealized expectation? Why does an unrealized expectation result in so much disappointment?

_____

_____

_____

_____

_____

What is the difference between an expectation, a goal, and a desire?

_____

_____

_____

_____

_____

How do you effectively handle expectations in your marriage?

> **LEADER:** This could be a good place to review the previous week's information on divine expectations, pointing out that expectations are a good thing, but they need to be realistic, biblical, and aimed not at getting what you want but helping you to grow as a couple in Christ.

1. __Trust__ **God with your spouse and marriage** (Proverbs 3:5; 16:9; Romans 8:28; Ezekiel 36:26–27).

> **LEADER: ILLUSTRATION BIG ROCKS:** You could bring the items for this example to the group. This familiar analogy pictures a jar, some big rocks, pebbles, and sand. If you put the

sand in followed by the pebbles, the big rocks don't fit. But if you start with the big rocks, then add pebbles, followed by sand, everything fits in the jar. Big rocks, the most important things, must come first. Walking with God: big rock. Marriage: big rock. Family: big rock. We have other important rocks like our jobs and friends and so on but keep the big rocks where they belong.[72]

Are you willing to surrender your expectations of your marriage and spouse to God and give thanks?

2. Pray together that ___God___ will help you both communicate your expectations to one another in an open, honest, loving way. Proactive communication: Matthew 7:7–8; Proverbs 13:12; Ephesians 4:29.

Pray and seek God, asking, "Do I trust God with my spouse and my marriage, even when it looks different than I thought it would?" Do you let unfulfilled expectations change the way you treat one another?

_____

_____

_____

_____

_____

72 "Prioritizing Your Life: Rocks, Pebbles and Sand," Mindful Practices, June 16, 2020, https://mindfulpractices.us/2020/06/16/prioritizing-your-life-rocks-pebbles-sand/.

3. Do not live by what you feel . Do not assume your spouse doesn't love/respect you when expectations are not met. Proverbs 3:5–6.

4. Have a plan for effectively facing different   expectations . Examples: "I thought we would save the bonus check" versus "I thought we would take a nice vacation with the bonus check," or "I thought we would go out Friday night with our friends" versus "I thought we would have a quiet dinner at home and watch TV," or "I thought we would get the garage in order on Saturday" versus "I thought we would go play tennis on Saturday."

How do these differences affect your marriage? How does what we learned about communication apply here? Proactive communication? Be intentional and strive for unity and compromise.

_____

_____

_____

_____

_____

LEADER: The Pygmalion effect is a term taken from a Greek myth about a sculptor who fell in love with a statue he carved. This is a form of self-fulfilling prophecy where a person's expectations influenced others without a clear reason. For instance, Harvard psychologist Robert Rosenthal conducted a study with an elementary principal.[73] Teachers were given names

---

73 "Pygmalion Effect: Expect the Expected," Academy 4SC, https://academy4sc .org/video/pygmalion-effect-expect-the-expected/.

of specific students who possessed high achievement capacity, or so the teachers were told. In fact, the students were selected randomly. Over the next two years, those students made greater progress academically, but not because they were gifted but because of the teacher's expectations. Applied to marriage, our expectations should be aimed at positive encouragement for growth in our spouse and our marriage that is realistic rather than arbitrary or unrealistic.

5. Speak __life__ over your spouse and marriage when you are discouraged (Hebrews 11:1).

Discuss the importance of your thoughts/declarations when discouragement sets in.

6. Decide _now_ how you will react when you realize your marriage (spouse) will not meet all of your expectations. Who can meet all of our needs (Philippians 4:19; Matthew 6:33; Isaiah 55:8)?

Discuss the importance of claiming/understanding/believing God meets all of our expectations/needs/desires and that our spouse is a gift from Him.

7. Take time to reflect as a couple on the spiritual __markers__ you have seen God provide up till now in your marriage.

Developing the practice of naming and remembering spiritual markers is a way to celebrate victories in your marriage.

LEADER: Every couple can think of specific spiritual markers in their marriage: answered prayer, provision in a time of need, helping you work through things in the past, and more. Share an example or two from your marriage.

Conclusion

Marriage is a blessing from the Lord to you. However, you WILL experience the unexpected with your spouse and marriage. How you handle the loss of your (dreams) expectations will determine the intimacy of your marriage and how you live out your faith. You probably will not have the exact marriage you always dreamt you would have, but if you surrender it to God, it will be an incredible blessing from the Lord above! (Jeremiah 29:11)

LEADER: You can conclude with the FRUIT ILLUSTRATION: If we walk up to an apple tree, what's going to be on it? Apples, not pears. Not oranges. If we want to produce the fruit of a healthy marriage, it will be consistent with the fruit of the Spirit in Galatians 5:22–23. The fruit of a Christian is clear in Galatians. The more you produce this fruit, the more your marriage will thrive!

Review and Application

1. How will you respond when your spouse or marriage does not meet your expectations? Do you commit to one another that you will discuss and talk through your expectations?

_____

_____

_____

_____

_____

2. What are the three most important desires and expectations you have for your spouse and marriage?

_____

_____

_____

3. What are some individual goals you have for yourself in your marriage?

_____

_____

_____

_____

_____

4. In faith, do you surrender your spouse and marriage to the Lord—even when it looks different than you expected?

_____

_____

_____

_____

_____

5. Discuss your ideal birthday, Christmas, anniversary, and other special occasions. Are those descriptions the same as your spouse? How are they different?

_____

_____

_____

_____

_____

6. Agree to be proactive in your communication of expectations.

_____

_____

_____

_____

_____

www.ingramcontent.com/pod-product-compliance
Lightning Source LLC
Chambersburg PA
CBHW071437090426
42737CB00011B/1692